Legends

Stories from Ireland's sporting greats

Edited by Patricia Scanlan

NEW ISLAND *Open Door*

LEGENDS
First published in 2022 by
New Island Books
Glenshesk House
10 Richview Office Park
Clonskeagh
Dublin, D14 V8C4
Republic of Ireland
www.newisland.ie

Many of the chapters of this book have been extracted from full-length autobiographies by the respective authors. Full information on these titles appears at the back of this book. Each extract featured in this book is abridged, and has been adapted into plain English for *Legends*.

The right of each contributor to be identified as the author of their respective chapter has been asserted in accordance with the provisions of the Copyright and Related Rights Act, 2000.

Print ISBN: 978-1-84840-875-3
eBook ISBN: 978-1-84840-876-0

British Library Cataloguing in Publication Data. A CIP catalogue record for this book is available from the British Library.

Typeset by JVR Creative India
Cover design by Jack Smyth, jacksmyth.co
Printed by Clays Ltd, Elcograf S.p.A., clays.co.uk

New Island Books is a member of Publishing Ireland.
10 9 8 7 6 5 4 3 2 1

Obstacles don't have to stop you. If you run into a wall, don't turn around and give up. Figure out how to climb it, go through it, or work around it.

– Michael Jordan

Just believe in yourself. Even if you don't just pretend that you do and, at some point, you will.

– Venus Williams

Also in the Open Door series:

And many more…

Contents

Dear Reader,

On behalf of myself and the whole team at New Island Books, I would like to welcome you to our first Open Door collection of sports stories.

Open Door is a series of books written in plain English for emerging adult readers.

We hope that you enjoy the book and that reading becomes a lasting pleasure in your life.

Warmest wishes,

Patricia Scanlan

Patricia Scanlan
Series Editor
New Island Open Door

Keith Earls

Keith Earls started out in senior rugby as a teenage star and during the course of his long career has become one of the most admired and respected players of his generation. A British and Irish Lion at the age of 21, he has won 93 caps for Ireland and played over 180 games in the famous red of Munster.

Yet, Earls has achieved these milestones while struggling with his mental health for most of his career. A number of crises brought him to the brink of early retirement from the game.

A native of Limerick city, Earls grew up in one of its most disadvantaged housing estates. Moyross was blighted by crime and violence which impacted the young Earls, but his natural talent and hard work brought him to the top of elite rugby union.

In this extract from his bestselling auto-biography, *Fight or Flight*, Earls recalls the problems he had at school and how he came back to education as an adult.

Fight or Flight

When John Broderick phoned to tell me I had the green light to start fifth year over in Saint Munchin's College, he asked me what subjects would I be choosing for my Leaving Certificate (Cert.). I told him to put me down for whatever Ger Sla was doing! I was not too fussy. I think he knew and I knew that I was not going back to get the points for Trinity College. Leaving Saint Nessan's meant giving up metalwork and woodwork, my two favourite subjects. I ended up doing biology and business instead. I would not be doing transition year. I would be going straight into fifth year.

I didn't bother with the books too badly in my last two years and they didn't bother me too badly either. My wife, Edel, says I got away with murder there. I was what you would call a part-time pupil. I did not cause any hassle and the teachers did not really hassle me. If we were taking turns in class to do a bit of reading out loud, the teacher would skip me. That was because I told them to skip me. I just refused point blank to read out loud because I did not get on well with words. I would struggle to read them properly.

When we had double French I would disappear altogether. If the teacher asked where I was going, I would say we have a big game at the weekend. I am going out to practise my kicking. OK so. And off I would go. Basically it was understood by everyone that I was in school not for the education but for the playing fields.

For the Leaving Cert I was supposed to be doing the subjects at ordinary level. But when the exams came I took the foundation papers where you just had to tick a load of boxes. You did not get any points in your Leaving for foundation level but you did get out of the exam hall fairly lively. I was gone after half an hour most days. Then for the biology exam I didn't bother showing up at all. Instead I went swimming with my old mates from Saint Nessan's at the Ardnacrusha bridge. They didn't do biology in Nessan's for the Leaving so the lads had the day off. I was outside the exam hall about to go in, when the phone rang. Sure I could not turn them down. It was a lovely hot day. What else would you be doing?

I would not recommend that attitude now. There is a reason why people say education is important. There is a reason why teachers tell you to pay attention in class. There is a reason why your parents tell you to study more. But if you do not understand those reasons at the time, there is less chance you will do it. And in fairness, studying is hateful to a lot of teenagers. It is unbelievably boring and annoying if you are not that way inclined. How are you supposed to do it if you do not have any aptitude for it? There were fellas in my class who had no aptitude whatsoever for sport. If they were forced to do it every day, it would be a horrible experience for them. It was a bit like that with me, except the other way round.

I was OK up to my Junior Cert. I passed all the subjects as far as I can remember. But after that, I could barely bring myself to open a book. It was torture. I could not concentrate. I had no feeling for it and not much interest in it. I came alive in the woodwork and metalwork classes. For the other classes it was like someone would switch me off inside. But then that left me without an important life skill. I do not know how the education system can fix that. Every person leaving school should be able to read and write properly but for a lot of kids, they do not suit the system. Or the system does not suit them. I was in that category.

Nearly fourteen years after my Leaving Cert, at a training camp in Portugal in January 2020, Andy Farrell arranged one-on-one meetings with the members of the squad. He was new in the job as Ireland head coach. He was establishing relationships, getting to know us and us getting to know him. In my session we got round to talking about life after rugby. Did I have any plans for afterwards? I told him I did not know what I was going to do. In passing I said that I was brutal at school. I could barely read or spell, so I would not be going into some sort of white collar, professional job. I had no qualifications like that. He showed a lot of empathy, the way he replied. Faz – Andy Farrell – is a working-class fella too. He didn't have the silver spoon growing up either. He said he knew lots of people who struggled with their reading and writing. It was more common than you would think. He said I should just practise it more. Even when sending text messages and emails, use the predictive text. The more you do it the better you will get at it.

A couple of weeks later we are on a weekend camp between Six Nations games. The staff have arranged one of their evening get-togethers for a bit of craic and relaxation. We are in a conference room in the hotel. Simon Easterby has put together a spelling competition. Big complicated words that the contestants have to try and get right. It is a forwards versus backs job, three forwards, three backs. And as he is picking them I'm going to myself, 'Jesus, do not pick me, Simon. Whatever the fuck you do, do not pick me.' Sure enough, he picks me.

You are not supposed to have a choice when there is messing like this going on. You are supposed to get up and face whatever prank is happening. But I refuse. The lads are all joking and egging me on but I say 'no, I am not going up there.' Thankfully Faz steps in. He remembered our chat from a few weeks earlier. So he just declares, 'Earlsy doesn't do spelling competitions', and that defuses the situation. Later Simon comes up to me privately and apologises, which is very nice of him. But there is no need because he just did not know.

Funny enough, I am not embarrassed by the episode at the time. I don't want to stand up and make a show of myself but I am not embarrassed either when Faz says I don't do spelling competitions. Ten years earlier I would have been mortified. But I am getting more confident in myself as I get older, and less self-conscious.

Since my diagnosis with bipolar in 2013, I have had to do a huge amount of work on myself to try and get to a better place. Out of that work came an appetite for self-improvement in general. If anything good has come out of it, it is getting to understand that you are not stuck with something forever if you don't want to be. You can change. You are not static. You don't have to be the victim of your circumstances or your conditioning. You can take control of your destiny, at least to some degree.

I am not saying it is easy. It is hard. You have to get the tools. You have to apply yourself. You have to put up with frustrations and setbacks and trial and error. Maybe that is why a lot of people cannot get out of the rut they are in. Because it is hard, it takes time and determination and discipline. That is where all the years of training in sport can help. It ingrains into you a discipline and a work ethic. When it came to my basic literacy skills, this was another project I had to take on. There was a path to self-improvement here too.

Obviously I needed to do it for my own sake. But there was another powerful motivation appearing as well. My daughter Ella May was starting to bring some homework back from school every day. And naturally she liked having Daddy to help her with it. And Daddy to his shame was not always able to help her. That is not a nice feeling. During lockdown last year the kids were homeschooling and I was trying to help out but in all honesty I was not able to help them much. Edel did most of it with them. It got to the stage where Ella May would be asking did I ever do anything in school? 'Did you learn anything at all?'

Well, I learned that it is probably not a good idea to go swimming the day of your Leaving Cert biology exam. It is probably not a good idea to finish school only being half-able to read and write. Being good at sport is not enough. At the time you think it is the perfect escape hatch out of the education system, but eventually you run into a cul-de-sac.

I remember one of the first times I signed an autograph. We were on a training camp in Cork and this fella came up to me with a jersey looking to get it signed. So I signed it 'Best

Whishes Keith Earls'. Then a few weeks later I saw the word written down somewhere and the correct spelling was 'Wishes'. When I realised my mistake, I felt unbelievably embarrassed and vulnerable. I could feel the cold sweat coming out of me.

This problem added to my paranoia too. I had to send emails and text messages every day, the same as everybody else. But I did not know where to put in full stops or when to start a new sentence. Something as simple as that made me really uptight for fear of making a show of myself. It is something that everyone takes for granted but that only makes it worse, if you are the fella who can not do it.

I would always be asking Edel to check the spelling of words before I would send a text or email. She has been my teacher here, as in so many things. Even in Saint Nessan's she'd be helping me with my homework, my maths and English in particular. Like for example I did not know how to put the address on an envelope properly. If I was asked to sign a message for a fan and post it, the first time Edel saw me doing it I wrote the full address across the envelope in one continuous line. She was looking at me. 'Do you not know that you go down line by line with the address?'

'No! That's news to me.' Then I put the stamp up in the left-hand corner instead of the right-hand corner! Now she was looking at me like I had two heads.

To this day if I am reading a book in bed I will be asking her to explain the meaning of words to me. She tells me I have come on in leaps and bounds the last few years. I probably have too, in fairness, but I still struggle with how words are spelled.

I have never got tested but I've a feeling I might have a touch of dyslexia. I was supposed to get tested for it last year but then the pandemic kicked in and the appointment was called off. I am no expert on it but from what I've learnt about it over the years, I would not be surprised if I was dyslexic. I'm going to get the test for it later this year hopefully. But letters and words are definitely a problem for me.

I leave letters out of words when I'm doing an email or any kind of writing. An 'e' or an 'n' or an 'a'. I have to revise what I have written and check with the dictionary. I keep a dictionary handy in my office. I will often just open a page and put my finger on a word and learn what it means and how to spell it correctly.

During the 2021 Six Nations I was asked to take part in a promo for one of our sponsors. It was basically a bit of video banter among a few players. Andrew Trimble and Donncha O'Callaghan were the hosts, myself and Tadhg Furlong were the guests. We were in the team hotel but in separate rooms because of the social distancing. We were hooked up to the lads on Zoom calls. It was one of those skits where you are asked light-hearted questions about your team mates. Who takes the longest to get dressed? Who is the best dancer? Who is in charge of the music? The catch for me was that you had to write your answers on a whiteboard with a marker. My answer for one of them was Shane Daly, my Munster team mate. Simple enough to spell but I left out the 'n' in 'Shane'. I realised my mistake and rubbed it out on the whiteboard and said his name instead. I knew how Shane is spelled and yet I still missed a letter. This happens to me regularly. It is why I think I might be dyslexic. I won't know until I get it properly tested but my life experience tells me there is something not quite right in my relationship with words on a page.

It's not holding me back as much as it used to. Of course it affected my confidence when I was younger, probably contributed to my shyness in some way. But I am pretty good at speaking now. I can stand up in a players' meeting and say what I want to say. I can do media interviews and talk shite with the best of them. I hope readers of this book will find it pretty simple to read. That is my intention.

I know there are a lot of kids who come from areas like mine who struggle at school. I am trying to use plain, basic English here in case a few of them might be interested in reading my story. If they leave school with literacy problems, I hope they realise they can get help. I'd hope they would not be too embarrassed about it to ask for help. It is a basic life skill. It is a basic human right, you could say.

I am sure I'm not the only professional sportsman who abandoned the books too young. It happens in soccer a lot. Fellas who are singled out for big things from an early age and put all their eggs in that basket. Then if they do not make it, they are kind of left stranded. The culture in pro rugby in Ireland is a bit different. Fellas are encouraged to continue with their studies or to go on various courses. It's a healthier environment because of that. In my case, that avenue was not really open to me. Or maybe it was, and I just did not see it. Anyway, I am making up for lost time now. I'm old in sporting terms but young in terms of the time I have ahead of me, touch wood. To answer Andy Farrell's question that day, I'm planning on going into business. As for my education, I will keep on turning up for class every day at the university of life.

Katie Taylor

Katie Taylor is a two-weight world champion boxer and the current undisputed lightweight champion. Following her victory over Delfine Persoon in 2019, she became one of only eight boxers in history (female or male) to hold all four major world titles in boxing – WBA, WBC, IBF, and WBO – at the same time.

In her amateur boxing career, Taylor won five consecutive gold medals at the Women's World Championships, gold six times at the European Championships, and gold five times at the European Union Championships. She was the flag bearer for Ireland at the 2012 London Olympics opening ceremony before going on to win an Olympic gold medal in the lightweight division.

In the following extract from her bestselling autobiography, *My Olympic Dream*, Taylor recounts that fateful match against the Russian boxer Sofya Ochigava.

The Final

Preparing for the Final

In the end it came down to two rounds. Over the next five minutes, I would either become an Olympic champion or I would lose in a major final for the first time in seven years. Sport has a habit of presenting things in bleak terms. For me the options were either failure or the fulfilling of a dream. There was nothing in between.

It was the biggest fight of my life and moments from the past stacked up in front of me. But the image that remained closest to me was the ten-year-old daddy's girl and the Olympic seed planted in my heart 16 years before. More than ever before, I had to believe that that seed was God-given. That it was my destiny. How could I believe anything else, since this dream had remained with me all these years from childhood until now, without ever fading.

Now, with my lifetime ambition hanging in the balance, the choice was a cruel, imperfect finish or the Olympic climax I longed for. I knew that the final against Sofya Ochigava would be a technical affair. They always are. For the long hours beforehand it was impossible to relax with the pressure bearing down. My stomach was churning.

I was trying to approach the Olympic final like any other fight. But no matter how much I tried to convince myself that this was just another fight, I knew that it was not. I knew that this was more than just a fight. I was not worried about my capacity to win. I was confident and I believed that I had the ability to beat the Russian. The struggle that day was controlling the nerves. I know I could not have handled it alone. Not without prayer.

I had boxed Ochigava three times in the past and I knew the fight was going to be close. So I had to prepare myself for a disciplined fight that could go right down to the last punch. I also had to focus on the tactics that Dad had devised after long and hard planning. My job was to execute that plan. Despite the pressure and regardless of the nerves.

Ochigava is a wily and very clever boxer. With the quality of their team and the coaches at her disposal in Russia, I was fully expecting the toughest fight of my life. In my mind, there was not anyone else in the Olympic competition that could have beaten Ochigava. What was vital was to stay calm and composed throughout. At the time, I did not realise how important that sort of thinking would be in the end. Or how vital it was in the first few moments of the final.

The Final Begins

It must have been for less than half a minute, but when the bell sounded for the start of the fight, although I was bouncing around and seemed to be moving well, I could not get going. I could see every punch that was coming, but I did not seem to be able to react to them in the way that I usually could. I had to step back and clear out of Ochigava's way to stop her from scoring. Meanwhile, I almost had to force my left hand to leave my face in order to get my jab going.

It seemed as though I was going through the motion of pushing out the shots, but there was a resistance. That first part of the fight seemed endless, but in real time it was no longer than the opening moments. This had never happened before. It was like there was a weight bearing down on my shoulders and my head was cloudy. I could not concentrate on what I needed to do. I am not sure if it was simply the pressure of the occasion or something deeper. Either way I thank God it lifted and my punches started to flow.

After the two minutes of the first round had come to a close, I was content to get back to my corner to see Dad and coach Zauri Antia. I felt the round had gone well despite the concerns of the opening moments. I thought I might have been a point up but the score was level at 2-2. I was satisfied with that. With that round behind me, I felt a lot more relaxed and happier than I was in the first 20 seconds.

It is amazing how moods can shift in a fight. Within seconds you can go from being in an uncomfortable struggle to being in charge and confident. That was what happened here, because by the break I really did feel sharper.

Round Two

For a lot of the time in the second round I was feinting (making a deceptive or distracting movement). Trying to make her react with some punches, so that I could then counter-punch her. It was tit-for-tat all of the time. A thinking match where we were both inviting the other to throw the first punch so that we could score with our own counter-attacks. Like all of our fights before, it was again turning into a game of chess more than a punching brawl. We were circling the ring and watching each other. Both of us waiting for the other to do something, to show their hand. There would be a flurry of activity as we both tried to snatch some scores and then it was back to the tense game of chess.

In retrospect, I was a bit too passive in round two and I paid the price. The score after the round was 4-3 to Ochigava. But I was not scared by the situation. I knew exactly what I had to do as I came back to my corner for a second time. I believed my dad when he told me I could pull back the lead from her. I just had to execute Dad's tactics better. Honestly, at this stage, I was still very confident. I was a point down, but we were composed.

I think that a few years ago, when I was in my early twenties, I might have become uptight about it and started to worry more about the clock ticking down. With my experience, I knew that trailing by one point or even two at this stage of the fight was absolutely nothing. It was part of the natural ebb and flow of any contest. I had been attacking from too far away during the second round and I got caught with a couple of shots. Towards the end of the round, I started to get back into it and I landed with a one-two. But I needed to get closer when I was trying to score. If I attacked her from too far out, it was too easy for her to time her counter punches.

Round Three

We had prepared for this situation well in advance of the final, back in the gym in Bray and in my training camps leading up to the Games. I went into the third round knowing that I could turn it around. Largely because Dad had hand-picked my sparring for this type of fight against a boxer like Ochigava. Before I came to London, I had been doing a lot of rounds with Eric Donavan. He is a brilliant Irish southpaw, and an established international boxer. He also came to the Olympic training camp in Assisi with me, so I could get as much practice as possible against his southpaw, counter-attacking style.

For years now, I have worked with some great-quality sparring partners in Ireland. Boxers who were better than the girls I was competing against in championships. I had sparred with double Olympic bronze medallist, Paddy Barnes, Olympic bronze flyweight, Michael Conlan, and even sometimes bantamweight silver medallist, John Joe Nevin. I was working with the best that Ireland has to offer. There is no doubt that being surrounded by this kind of talent has played a part in my own success.

That ability to raise my level of performance had rarely been more crucial than it was now. I did exactly that in the defining third round against Ochigava. By the end of the two minutes, I had overturned the deficit. I was now two points ahead overall after my best phase in the fight, with the score reading 7-5. I had to be more aggressive in the third round, but not in the same way, I was against Jonas in the quarter-finals. This fight required a more controlled and tactical aggression. I was getting closer before letting off my combinations, and then avoiding her attacks at the same time. I won the round 4-1. It was the crucial point in the contest and entirely changed the fight around in my favour. I knew then that she was going to have to move out of her normal pattern and attack me more in the last round if she wanted to win. I would have to be ready for her.

Round Four

The scales had tipped. She now had to chase me and everyone in the stadium knew she would be coming. It would make for a tense two minutes. I could not give away any cheap shots. One good shot could change the momentum and I could not let that happen during the final round. The last thing I wanted to give her now was a glimmer of hope.

I kept her on her toes all of the time during that last round with a series of feints. The two-point advantage was no more than a small cushion. But it had been clear throughout the whole week that the final round was generally win-or-bust for the chasing boxer as they tried to claw back the score. I knew that a bad spell of ten seconds could have changed the whole course of the fight. So it was probably the most cautious round of my life. I was reluctant even to exchange punches in case the judges saw her punches and not mine. I tried to stay out of reach, pumping out my left any time she stepped into range.

At the end of the fourth round, the bell sounded. I looked across at Dad and Zauri in the corner and asked 'Is it me?' I did not know what the score was, but I was sure that it was close. It is not always easy to guess what way the judges are seeing a fight. Important incidents in the round raced through my mind. The couple of times we exchanged combinations, what way did the judges score them? What about when I slipped on the canvas, did they score that? Did I do enough to hold her off for the win?

Usually the judges' decision is announced quickly once the fight is over. But this was not one of those days. It seemed to be taking ages for them to make their announcement. The delay did not help my nerves. Dad kept reassuring me that the decision was going my way and that there was no way I lost the last round by two points, but the longer it went on, the more doubts ballooned in my head.

Then I thought the decision was going to a count-back, which is what happens when the judges score the fight as a tie by the usual scoring method. We were waiting so long that Dad had stopped reassuring me and I think even he began to wonder if it was going to go to a count-back. Then the decision could be something of a lottery.

You could hear a pin drop in the stadium as we waited. The crowd had fallen from megaphone levels of uproar to a complete silence. Nobody knew what was happening. Finally, they began to announce the decision: 'And the winner of that contest by a score.' I'm waiting to hear the words 'in the red corner', but before I could make out what was said, the crowd had erupted in pandemonium at the announcement. Then I felt the referee begin to raise my right arm, and I knew it was me. I was the Olympic champion!

Ronnie Delany

Ronnie Delany was born in Arklow, County Wicklow, but grew up in Sandymount, Dublin. He won a gold medal in the 1,500 metres running event at the 1956 Summer Olympics in Melbourne, Australia. The following extract from his autobiography, *Staying the Distance*, recounts that famous race

He went on to win a bronze medal at the 1958 European Athletics Championships in Stockholm. He retired from competitive athletics in 1962, yet remains one of Ireland's most recognisable Olympians.

Staying the Distance

In the early evening of 19 November we arrived in the Olympic city to a tumultuous welcome from many Irish-Australian societies. There were Irish pipers and colleens, dressed in national costume, on hand for the occasion. The Irish down under were thrilled to see their old country represented in the Games. They extended to us the heartiest of good luck and best wishes. We arrived at the Olympic Village and settled in immediately. We were tired and needed to rest up after our long journey. But before going to bed we raised an Irish flag outside our quarters.

As it so happened, it was the largest flag put up. The other nations had standard sized ones. Before we knew it every newspaper man in the village was outside photographing it. It caused a sensation. Next morning matters were put right. Or wrong, depending on which way you look at it, when the camp commandant came along with the proper sized flag. He took our big one down and went through a formal ceremony of unfurling the new flag.

My first days in the village were filled with meeting members of other nations' teams whom I already knew. It was great seeing my teammates from Villanova, Charlie Jenkins and Phil Reavis were both competing, of course, for the U.S. (United States). Charlie had a store of information on my opponents. He had done some research for me. He told me Landy was having trouble with his legs. Bailey was having trouble with his nose, and that the one-two threat of the Australians was considered weakened. Rozsavolgyi and Tabori of Hungary, and the British team of Hewson, Wood and Boyd were all thought highly of by the experts. The tension in the village itself was electric. All about me were lean, strained faces with eyes sunk deep from the long hours of training. Everywhere there was talk of who would win this and that. All of which, if you listened to it, would only make you twice as nervous and tense.

For the most part, I kept to myself and my Irish teammates.

Shortly after my arrival in the village I met the three Britons, Hewson, Wood and Boyd. Despite our centuries of differences, we Irish and British were friendly to one another. They were all talk about who was going to win the 1,500 metres and mentioned everyone's name, practically. I gathered they were in a state of high tension and when they asked me who I thought would win I announced blandly, 'Myself.' I might as well have insulted the Queen, it had such an effect on them. One of them actually screamed. The last thing they wanted to hear apparently was one of their competitors saying he was going to win. Admittedly, I said it more out of bravado than in belief I could do it. But in Cold Wars terms, the Irish had put one over on the British again.

On 22 November the opening ceremony of the 1956 Olympics took place. Teams from 67 nations paraded into the Olympic Stadium before a crowd of over 100,000. Even if one were never to win an Olympic medal, the memory of the opening ceremony would last a lifetime. Somehow every athlete I have spoken to on the subject has expressed the same sentiment. There is something very special, historic and significant in being sent by your country to an Olympic Games. And this realisation comes to you as you participate in the opening ceremony, before the eyes of the world.

The taking of the Olympic oath. The fanfares of trumpets. The choirs. The lighting of the Olympic flame. The releasing of the doves of peace carrying their message that the Games are on, all combine to make a great spectacle. And an undying impression on the mind of the participants. I was proud of my heritage and my native land, as I stood erect in the Olympic Stadium, a privileged member of the Irish team.

I was not due to run until a week later in the preliminary heats of the 1,500 metres. I did not go to the track and field events for more than an hour each day. I found the tension too great. I had the thrill of seeing Charlie Jenkins win the 400-metre crown and believed I could have won the high jump, with my exultant leap, as he breasted the tape. The days flew by and I was preparing myself mentally for the task ahead. I reasoned I was as fit and strong as anyone in the race. I was faster than most over a half mile or quarter, and a four-minute miler to boot. I believed I had it in me to win.

I was almost alone in this opinion, except for my coach, my family and my closest friends. No one looked for the reason for my defeats. The fact that I was spiked in Paris and out of training for three weeks was completely ignored. In retrospect, it is probably a good thing not to be favoured.

The heats of the 1,500 metres were held on Thursday, but qualifying for the final turned out to be a mere formality. The first four in each of the three heats went on to the final on Saturday. I strolled home in third place in my heat comfortably, behind Merv Lincoln of Australia and Ken

Wood of Great Britain. The much favoured Tabori of Hungary was in the fourth spot. Rozsavolgyi, the world record holder, was eliminated.

The final was wide open despite Landy's position as favourite. There were four other four-minute milers in the field besides myself – Landy, Hewson, Tabori and Nielsen – and I was younger than any of them. Halberg and Scott of New Zealand were comparatively inexperienced. Lincoln of Australia had probably run too fast in winning his heat. Richtzenhain of Germany and Jungwirth of Czechoslovakia were unknown quantities. Of the two other Britons in the race, Wood was considered a dark horse, but Boyd hardly seemed up to the class of the race.

Friday was spent resting and relaxing as far as possible under the trying circumstances. Every moment my mind was turning over analysing my opponents. It was virtually impossible to decide on the form of the field. Finally I settled to my own satisfaction that Landy was still my greatest threat. Hewson was the next most likely to succeed in beating me to my life's ambition. I also considered the possibility of an outsider of the inspired sort who suddenly appears in Olympic finals and performs way above himself, running off with the laurels. It was this sort of inspiration I was hoping for myself.

The day I had lived for dawned bright and warm. It was difficult to remain calm but I tried as best I could, for I knew every moment of anxiety used up valuable energy. I resigned myself quietly to the will of God. I prayed not so much for victory but the grace to run my best. When I arrived at the Olympic Stadium I immediately went to the warm-up area for the 'roll call' and to prepare for my race. One of the first people I met was Charlie Jenkins. In spite of the seriousness of the occasion for me, he could not restrain himself from bursting into laughter when he saw the anxiety written all over my face. I will always remember what he said to me. 'Man, I know what you are going through. I am sure glad my ordeal is over'. He could well laugh with his Olympic gold medal already secured. And with the possibility of another before him in the 1,600-metre relay final, later in the day.

Before I fully realised it, the race was called. We were marched single file through a dark tunnel. Out into the sudden glaring brightness of the Olympic oval, before 100,000 partisan fans ready to cheer on their hero, John Landy. Yet, as we moved across the stadium toward the starting area, John came over to me and wished me good luck. It was typical of this great sportsman.

It is funny how even in life's most serious moments one cannot help being amused by some little detail. The three British athletes were moving around as if they were glued together. All ashen faced and looking as if they were going to the gallows rather than the starting line. I remember reprimanding myself and thinking I would not be so amused if one of these Englishmen were ahead of me at the finish.

There was one false start. We were lined up again. The pistol fired and the Olympic 1,500-metre final was on. In a crowded field of twelve, one had to avoid trouble and I did this by running at the back of the pack. After 400 metres in 58.9 seconds, Halberg was leading, with Hewson nicely placed and a bunched field right behind. Lincoln took the lead at the 800-metre mark in 2:00.3, with his fellow Australian Landy last and myself just in front of him. At the bell the entire field was fantastically gathered within a mere six yards. Lincoln, Hewson and Richtzenhain were in the lead. I was back in tenth place but I was very much in touch with the leaders.

The pace at this stage of the race was not troubling me. I knew I could not afford to allow anyone to break into a lead at this vital stage of the race so I moved out wide to allow myself a clear run. About 350 yards from the finish. As we went down the back stretch for the last time, Hewson was forging away in the lead. Suddenly Landy sprinted. I reacted immediately, slipping into his wake, following him as we passed the struggling figures of the other competitors. I knew if I were to win I would have to make one, and only one, decisive move. I restrained myself as long as possible, and about 150 yards from the finish I opened up with everything I had.

Within ten yards I was in the lead and going away from the field. I knew nobody was going to pass me, for my legs were pumping like pistons, tired but not going to give in to anybody. My heart swelled with joy as I approached the tape, ten feet clear of the rest of the field. As I burst through I threw my arms wide in exultation. I could hardly believe I had won. My eyes swelled with tears, and I dropped to my knees in a prayer of thanksgiving. John Landy, who finished third, came over to me, helped me to my feet and warmly congratulated me. The Australian crowd was showing its sportsmanship by generously applauding me.

It was the happiest day of my life.

Gavin Bazunu

Gavin Bazunu played with Shamrock Rovers underage football teams. At the age of just sixteen, he was unexpectedly handed his first team debut in 2018. The teenage goalkeeper played just four league games and two Europa League qualifiers for Rovers. But his performances marked him out as an exceptional talent.

In 2019 Bazunu was signed by Manchester City for a transfer fee of €500,000. In 2021, he made his debut for the Republic of Ireland as a nineteen-year-old. He is the youngest goalkeeper to play a senior international with the Boys in Green. In 2022 he was signed by Southampton Football Club.

In the following extract from the book *From Ringsend to Tallaght*, he recalls his early days with Shamrock Rovers.

From Ringsend to Tallaght

The first game I ever attended was the Shamrock Rovers match against Real Madrid in the club's first season in Tallaght. I was seven years old. You never forget that first game. It was brilliant. Rovers did really well. I remember the team playing that game had Stephen Rice, Pat Flynn and Shane Robinson. Shane has been a huge influence on my career and has been great to me, as Rovers' academy director.

I started at the club when I was really young. I was probably six when I started with Rovers, my first football club. I was playing with a team that was a year ahead of my age. I played up until Under-10 and we did quite well but the team folded for some reason. I went to Leicester Celtic and then on to Mount Merrion for a year. I did well. I enjoyed it, but it was difficult to get lifts there as it was quite far from my house. At the end of that season I went to Knocklyon. That was more local for me and much easier for my parents to drop me there after school and collect me. I broke my leg during that season so I didn't really play that much. After that, I came back to Rovers at Under-14 level.

I didn't really like playing in goal when I was younger. I loved playing outfield. I reckon I played in nearly every position. But as I was moving around those clubs I found I was much, much better in goals. As I played in goal more and more, it really grew on me. I liked it as I was getting better all the time and I stuck with it. I was always quite tall for my age. From 12 or 13 I started to grow really quickly.

I always wanted to finish my Leaving Cert and never wanted to go away too early. I think it is a big thing to have your Leaving Cert behind you. In August 2017, I started with Ashfield College, as part of Rovers' academy education partnership. I started training with the first team. From the start of 2018, I was in and around the first team match day squad. Warming up, sitting in the stands, being around the lads in the dressing room and getting used to the environment.

For my debut, in the 5-0 win over Bray Wanderers in Tallaght Stadium in June 2018, I only found out I was playing about an hour and a half before kick-off, in the team meeting. I was really nervous but it did not really feel all that different. I had been warming up for a couple of months ahead of matches so it was a routine at that stage. Obviously it was nerve wracking but it was a great opportunity as well.

I never really expected my debut to come so early. I was delighted when it did. I tried to take my chance as much as I could. It was fast and loud in the stadium. It was different than I expected but I felt comfortable as soon as I got my first touch of the ball. It just felt like any other game.

My parents and my brother were there that day and they were really delighted and a bit surprised. My brother loved it. He loved being able to see me playing on the pitch instead of watching players he would not have known. My parents are a big influence. My mum is always supporting me in my football. My dad is a big football fan, and a huge Shamrock Rovers fan now. He played a lot of football back in Nigeria, before he came over to Ireland around the year 2000.

Going down on the team bus to play Cork City, Jose Ferrer (Rovers' goalkeeping coach) was showing me clips. We looked through them together, looking at the different set pieces and corners, free kicks and penalties. I saw their penalties and I made my decision. If there was a penalty I would go to my right. Jose was brilliant for me. He helped me improve so much. When Alan Mannus signed, he provided a lot of knowledge for me, because of the experience he had from playing for so long. It was great to be able to learn from such a good goalkeeper.

I see goalkeepers like Edison, Allison, ter Stegen and Donnarumma. They are the modern day goalkeepers who are brilliant with their feet. You have to be so versatile. You have to be almost as good as the outfield players with your feet. I really love seeing goalkeepers like Edison and Allison in the Premier League who are able to do that.

It was a big step up, making my international debut, but I tried to use some of those previous experiences of playing in Europe with Rovers. And getting a lot of first team games with Rochdale, on loan. That experience gave me confidence going into the game.

I have been training at a first team level from such a young age. I was training with the Rovers first team when I was 14. Being around a men's first team dressing room gave me the confidence and understanding of how to speak to your team mates. I understand what the experienced players want in their goalkeeper. Whether you are young or old, they want to know that there is someone behind them who has the confidence to tell them where and when to be.

I was nervous before the first game for Ireland but I didn't feel any pressure. As soon as the whistle went it was like any other game. I felt comfortable and I made sure to stick to my little key things, like be loud, be brave, communicate. Once I have those things, it feels like any other game.

Philly McMahon

Philly McMahon was a mainstay of the All-Ireland winning Dublin Gaelic football team from 2008 until his retirement from inter-county football in 2021. An entrepreneur and social activist, he owns and operates a number of businesses, including three gyms and Fit Food, a meal preparation service. Since losing his brother, John, Philly has become an outspoken advocate for many addiction and mental health initiatives.

In this extract from his award-winning book, *The Choice*, he remembers the 2011 All-Ireland Senior Football Championship, when Dublin won their first All-Ireland title since 1995.

The Choice

I want to stop.

My mind sends the message, but something slows it down as it goes from my brain to my legs. Rust. By the time I jam on the brakes and turn, I have only gone a step or two too far, but that is far enough. It feels like every eye in Croke Park is on me, wondering what is going on. But the reality is that it all happens in a split-second and nobody even notices.

Anyway, they are all watching Colm Cooper as he curls the ball over the bar. The green and gold jerseys are on their feet again.

Fuck. What am I even doing here?

Into the championship rounds and Kerry have their foot on our neck. They are four points up with seven minutes to play. Shoulders back and chests out. Two years on, we are not startled earwigs any more, but it is still looking like the same old story. Another chapter in the tale of the nearly men.

Many Dubs (people from Dublin) draw their family tree from roots on Hill 16 and the moments that have been shared there between generations of fathers and sons and mothers and daughters. Standing side by side in their usual spots, they are fighting a losing battle against their worst instincts now, and already starting to wonder about what might have been. There is always next year.

There will be plenty of time for everyone to tell us how we got it wrong. Good but not good enough, they will say. There for the taking and they could not get over the line again. Second best. Maybe that is their level.

I know that Cooper is going to sell me that dummy. There is nothing wrong with how I am reading the game, but once he cuts in, all I can do is throw out a hand in hope and I am forced to face the truth. It is mad how deeply you can look inside yourself in those moments. How nothing else registers, even though there are 29 other lads out there fighting with you and against you. And 82,000 spectators hanging on every move. For weeks, I have been telling Pat Gilroy that I am fit and ready. And I have convinced myself, but it is obvious that after two months out injured, I am an inch or two short of where I need to be. And in an All-Ireland final, inches are the difference between blocks and scores.

But you recognise that and accept it. Then you have to forget it. That play is over. When the next ball comes, I will back myself, same as always. And maybe that is what people don't see when they look at us and they question our heart and our stomach for the battle. This Dublin team has learned its lessons the hard way. Once the final whistle blows, there will be nothing more we can do, but until then, we are not done fighting.

In an instant, everything changes. A quick free from midfield and Alan Brogan is turned and running at them. Kev McManamon is on his shoulder. Give it, give it, give it. Alan waits and pops it but the Kerry men are standing guard. Three of them blocking the path to goal, warning Kev. Do not even think about it. He is like me, thrown in from the bench in the second half with only one thing on his mind. Make an impact. If he sticks the ball over the bar and gets us back to within three, he will have done that.

Michael Darragh MacAuley is sprinting through in support. Bernard Brogan is on the edge of the square, crying out for the pass. But Kev is at full tilt and he has other ideas. He drops his shoulder and the goal opens up for him. Then it is all about keeping a cool head.

The Kerry net ripples and the Hill's fading dreams are transformed from a flicker to a roar. For 16 years those fans have waited for a Dublin All-Ireland, 16 years of doubts and scars wiped away with a goal. A giddiness rushes in to take their place. There are fans my age who can barely remember the glory days of 1995. I barely remember them myself. The

Dubs are giants of Gaelic football, for sure, but despite everyone's best efforts, they have been half-asleep for most of my life.

Nobody is nodding off now. The whole stadium is electrified and we are the ones feeding off the energy. Just two minutes earlier we looked tired, nothing left in the tank after an hour of hounding Kerry around the park. And even with that, it looked like we were still going to come up short. Now they are the ones backing up and making mistakes, and we are on the balls of our feet, trying to pick our shots.

Now you will see what we are about.

We win another turnover and get the ball moving quickly again. Kev Nolan has the freedom of Dublin out on the Hogan Stand side, and kicks one of the scores of the day. All square. Then Bernard squeezes over a point to put us into the lead with two minutes left. All around us, the noise and the energy levels have gone up another notch. But the stakes are totally different and there is a nervousness running through it. Hands on heads and on hearts, and then Kieran Donaghy kicks a point to draw Kerry level with 30 seconds to play.

If it goes to a replay, we will be back here to do it all again in two weeks. But the referee signals that there are two additional minutes to be played and one team is bound to get a chance in that time. We just need to make sure that it is us.

Kev Mc goes down, tripped by a loose leg, and the whistle goes. We have a free, 40 metres from goal, a little to the right of the posts. Kev is still on the ground, hanging onto the ball as if it was the Sam Maguire itself. They are already waving Stephen Cluxton to come up and kick it. The All-Ireland on the line and he jogs out of his goal past me, the coolest man in the house. All anybody else can do is watch.

As Clucko places the ball, you cannot hear the difference between the curses and the prayers. It is all just noise, and it gets louder with each step back that he takes. But then he strikes it, and for a fraction of a moment after the ball leaves his foot, it is like somebody has turned the sound all the way down to zero. A deep breath multiplied by thousands. Some in hope and some in fear.

That moment of stillness is so brief that it barely registers before it is swallowed up again. There is a pocket of Dublin fans on the Hill who are in the perfect position to judge the flight of the ball and they are the first to react. It is a sound like nothing I have ever heard in my life. Starting from the terrace and wrapping its way around the four sides of the stadium. Defeats in sport do not last forever, but a little bit of every disappointment stays with you, bottled up. Now it is bursting free all around me, uncontrollable joy. The stands shake to their foundations. Down on the pitch, it is so loud that my head is shaking too.

We have played the two additional minutes but the game is still not over. Kerry have taken the restart quickly and they are trying to work it down the field. Clucko is sprinting back towards his goal in case they get to within shooting range.

I have made the mistake in the past of wishing for a game to be over. I swore to myself that I would never let it happen again. But this is every dream I have ever had and it is about to come true.

Blow it up, ref. Blow it up.

He does, and the place erupts all over again. A minute ago, Croke Park was a chessboard, every move on the pitch so precise. Now it is a blur of sky blue and navy. The happiest kind of chaos. We run, even though we have nowhere to run to. We cry, even though we are happier than we have ever been. Arms arrive out of nowhere and pull us into hugs. There are no words, only roars of pure emotion.

By the time we go up to lift the Sam Maguire, I am banjaxed. Not from the game, but from all of the running around and jumping up and down celebrating. I am sure I am not the only one.

Michael Darragh gets pulled aside for an interview by RTÉ. I do not know how any player can be expected to explain those feelings. What we could possibly say that would even begin to scratch the surface, but that does not stop people from asking. He is buzzing so much he can hardly get the words out. 'Unbelievable,' he keeps saying. 'Unbelievable.' He is right, it is unbelievable, but it will be a while before we let him live that interview down.

I am over at the Hogan Stand. I know my parents are in there somewhere, near the Ard Chomhairle box and the steps. I am scanning through the smiles of different shapes and sizes. Every one of them with their story about this day and what it means to them.

I find the one I want. It is not difficult. My dad is hard to miss at the best of the times. A big man and a tough man. I run to the railings where he is standing, bawling his eyes out. My mam and my sister Kellie are a few rows back, still in their seats, but Dad has made his way down to the front of the stand. In 24 years, I do not think I have ever seen him cry, but he is hugging me and telling me how proud he is, the tears rolling down his face onto my jersey.

Those first few moments are special. Just us and our families, before we step out of the bubble and the phones start buzzing. And the rest of the world arrives to join the party. This is why we do it. Every hour we put in when we train, every sacrifice we make, it is exhausting, but it is a privilege. We are the lucky ones who get to lace up our boots when everyone is watching. But that Dublin jersey is not ours. It belongs to the communities that shaped us, the clubs that trained us, the families that raised us. Our success will always be theirs too.

Dad eventually lets go of me.

I am an All-Ireland champion and I will have these memories forever. It is almost perfect.

All that is missing is John.

Sonia O'Sullivan

Sonia O'Sullivan is one of the greatest sporting figures Ireland has ever produced. Her career as a track and field athlete saw her competing at the highest international levels for over a decade. She turned in world-class times in events ranging from the 1,500 metres to the marathon, capped by World Championship gold in the 5,000 metres in 1995 and Olympic silver in the same event in 2000.

In the following extract from her autobiography, *Sonia: My Story*, O'Sullivan recalls her experience at the Barcelona Olympics in 1992.

Barcelona Olympics 1992

Lollipops. Christmas parties. Little things like that were the incentives that drew me in. Trips. The fun of it. We would travel to Dublin on the train, for races in Santry, or Belfield. When the ticket collector came around, a gang of us would hide in the loo. We would leave maybe two of our accomplices with the three tickets we had bought between us. All those wet days. All those evenings running in sodden fields after school. All the rivalries and all the sessions. All the medals thrown into boxes, and all the defeats brooded over for weeks. All of that leads to here. To an Olympic final. And all the little things you bring to it to make you think that you have an edge. That this is your time.

A few moments ago, just as we walked to the start line with 65,000 people in the stadium suddenly attentive towards us, I glanced up and I noticed the Olympic flame burning orange against the purple night. And it struck me for the first time – I mean really hit more than anything else – that this is the Olympics. This is the dream.

Down on the track, this can be a lonely thought to find yourself holding on to, just before the start of the biggest race of your life. But the night was playing tricks. I looked away from the flame and across the great wall of faces and I locked eyes with, of all people, my father. Dad grinned at me. The whole world watching but we locked for a moment. This is the Olympics but, kid, it is only a race. The gun cracks and we shoot off at first like mildly startled animals, jockeying for position and throwing shapes at one another. It's slow. You would think that Olympic finals would be run at full pace. That the person who could run the quickest would dictate that pace. But we are cagey and we each have our strengths.

In the 1988 Olympic final, Mary Decker Slaney went for the slash-and-burn tactic, pushing everybody out at world record pace for the first 1,000 metres. She was still in front at the halfway mark but she had not shaken the pack. At 2,000 metres my Villanova college mate, Vicki Huber, went past Mary Decker Slaney. Then Yvonne Murray went past. Then Tetyana Samolenko. (now running under her married name, Tetyana Dorovskikh). They kept pouring past Mary Decker Slaney. The medallists and the fourth and fifth-placed girls all improved their personal best times by at least seven seconds. Mary Decker Slaney finished ninth for her troubles. There is no way anybody is going to make the same mistake tonight.

So here in Barcelona, up on the hill they call Montjuic, Alison Wyeth goes to the front for a bit. I think nothing of it. The pace doesn't get any faster just because Alison is leading us. The big guns are not impressed or worried. So I stay tucked in with the pack. I have certain cards in my hands. Everyone else has other cards, their strengths. We play them when we see fit. The first move that interests us is when, coming down the back straight towards the bell for the last lap, Yvonne Murray moves to the front. I have been watching Yvonne all along through. She is the

European Champion and, for me tonight, the favourite. 500 metres left and Yvonne has to go now. She got a bronze in Seoul and she ran 8:29.02 in that final. She has not got a devastating kick at the finish, so Yvonne needs to go now if she is to get on the podium.

When she makes her move it sets a flag waving in my head. I have been waiting for this. Yvonne plays her card and I raise her. I skip away from the pack and fasten myself on to Yvonne's frail shoulders. See ya, suckers. And suddenly, very quickly, I realize that Yvonne's cards are all on the table and that she has been holding nothing. She goes. I go. And I realize with over 300 left that she is dead. Running on empty. The two of us are not leaving the field behind. I am practically bumping into Yvonne's shoulder blades.

Nerves get to her, I think. Yvonne put the pedal to the floor before she was supposed to. I accelerated, just to stay with her. Now she is out of fuel. With 300 metres to go she has all but stopped. She has nothing left, and suddenly I find myself in the lead, not knowing what to do. Another fine mess!

I do not have the confidence to be out here. I just run as hard as I can, but deep down I know that I am running scared. Waiting for the worst. We had been coming on to the start of the back straight of the final lap when Yvonne evaporated into the night and left me alone, out in front of an Olympic field. About 150 metres away from my comfort zone. It is too soon, but it is too exciting also. The crowd are clapping in rhythm, trying to urge somebody to make a move. So I go with it. I make a push. Maybe I have enough. Maybe fear, adrenaline and innocence will push me home. Now the walls are making so much noise. All around me this massive bowl is coming alive. People are on their feet. Flashbulbs are popping. The hot lava excitement has just spilled over and down on to the red oval where we have been playing cat and mouse.

I go for it. Flat out. Push. Push. Push. Down around the last bend. Legs stretching as far as they can go, arms pumping. I cannot hear the footfalls behind me. I cannot glance up at the immense screen. I cannot see the posse. But I can tell from the noise washing over us that I am not escaping them on this last bend. They are reeling me in.

We come around on to the final straight. We are beyond thought and tactics now. Our guts are busting, our hearts are pumping. I can feel their breaths on my shoulders. There is just 100 metres to an Olympic medal. 90 metres. Just down that track. I can see glory … No!

It is all over. I was out in front, still running, but in reality a dead girl walking. Out in front, with the world watching, and just asking questions. Why am I here? What am I doing? I could not handle the answers. I had run a young athlete's race. The whole Olympics experience overtook me when I had planned it the other way around. I was racing against the same people on the same size track as I always did, but next thing I knew I was getting passed. A sucker's race.

I knew it would come, but still I was not ready for it. When they come from behind they have it all. They can see how you are going. They can make all the judgements. I got passed and they disappeared. If I had run for a medal or held my head 200 or 300 metres back I would have had a chance, but I went for it. I went crazy, gambled and lost. When they pass you like this, you are dead. Really just dead.

So Romanova steams past on my right. A dark blur. I am 85 metres now to an Olympic silver I know I will not get. I hardly have time to think or react when Dorovskikh goes through on my left. They go almost in unison, reacting to each other. I know without needing to look that I do not exist for them anymore.

My legs have no more power. Angela Chalmers in her red-and-blue Canadian outfit goes past me on the right, and suddenly in the space of 20 metres, my story has changed. Gold. Silver. Bronze. Fourth. Footnote. The loneliest corner at the party.

There is a picture of that moment when I died. People used to come up to me and ask me to sign it. Romanova, Dorovskikh and Chalmers have all gone past and my face is just like that painting, 'The Scream' by Edvard Munch. I look like I am crying but I am just screaming. I had just watched my death.

Afterwards my dad cries. I cry. Many tears get spilled, but hey, hey, hey, this is a journey. It is ongoing. I have travelled. Five years ago, I was a seventeen-year-old kid with a big mop of hair and I surprised everyone, myself included, by galloping away with the senior Irish cross-country title at a race in Killenaule.

The TV people were there and they asked me, 'What now?' I stood there in my black-and-yellow Ballymore-Cobh singlet and I probably should have said, 'Now? A fish burger and chips in Mandy's, please.' Or, 'Now? I'm going to do my maths homework.'

But I said, 'I'd like to run in the Olympics but sure I'll take each day as it comes.'

Now I am under the stand in Montjuic. I have run in the Olympics. It's over. Fourth place leaves you with nothing to hang round your neck, but I have run in the Olympics and I know that it was not enough. Now I have to do the second part. Continue the journey. I have to take each day as it comes. Fourth place. I run out into the night with Kim, warming down as we jog back towards the Olympic village.

I hardly know this man, but Kim listens and I talk. I unravel. I tell him I screwed up. I tell him that I got it wrong. I tell him I was so close. This close.

He tells me that I just got into the wrong place at the wrong time. He tells me that I am 22. He tells me that in my career the starter's pistol just sounded. Journey. Journey. Journey. He lets me know that fourth is enough for today. Fourth place lets me reach my arm into the big box and pull out a lollipop. I have a career now and it is on the track. One day at a time.

A.P. McCoy

A.P. McCoy was born in County Antrim in 1974, and rode his first winner in 1992. In 1996, he was crowned champion jockey for the first time, and he held the title every year until his retirement in 2015. He received an OBE (Order of the British Empire award) in 2010, a year after riding his 3,000th winner. He was the first jockey to be named BBC Sports Personality of the Year. He lives with his wife, Chanelle, and children, Eve and Archie, in Berkshire, in the United Kingdom.

In the following extract from his autobiography, he remembers an exciting win at the 2010 Grand National.

Note: The horses' names are in bold text.

That's Pushing It

For the 2010 Grand National, I got to the course early and took things easy. I felt relaxed. No major pressure, no panic. I did not think that I was any more or less relaxed than other years. But maybe I was a little more relaxed, because I did not think that I had a great chance of winning the race.

Actually, everyone was very relaxed in the parade ring beforehand. J.P. McManus is always quiet before a race. He does not want to get too involved, especially for the bigger races. He just wished me luck. Jonjo O'Neill, the handler, is quiet as well. We did not have too many tactics. He never ties me to instructions. We discuss the race. What might happen. But he leaves it up to me to see how the race develops. Which is how it should be. If you are tying a jockey to strict instructions, if you are not allowing him to work it out for himself, you are employing the wrong jockey. Then he legged me up. I did get butterflies when I got to the start though. I always do. You can't help but get carried away by the atmosphere.

If you do not get butterflies as you circle at the start before the Grand National, you are doing the wrong thing.

Don't Push It was getting butterflies too. He was sweating like mad. I did not mind too much. It is usually a bad sign when a horse sweats up before a race. It usually means that he is anxious, too anxious to run his race. But **Don't Push It** always sweated up. It was just him. I took my feet out of the irons and patted him down the neck. Jonjo had inserted a pair of earplugs into his ears, just to insulate him a bit from the noise, to help him relax. We did not want him wearing them in the race as we had not declared them. But I wanted to leave it until as near to start time as possible before I took them out. I did not want him getting buzzed up too early.

I looked up at the big screen to check on the betting.

It is no harm knowing what is being backed in the race. What else is fancied. What your dangers might be. I could not believe what I was seeing. **Don't Push It** was plummeting in price: 20/1, 16/1, 14/1, 12/1.

The starter asked us to line up. A couple of lads started charging towards the tape. I could see that **King Johns Castle** and Paul Carberry were way behind us, and there were a couple of other horses that were not ready. We circled for another minute or so. Then the starter called us in again. **King Johns Castle** was still being a bit reluctant, but this looked like it could be it.

'Come on then!'

As the starter released the tape, the crowd roared behind us.

I was in the middle of the track and towards the rear, crossing the Melling Road on the way to the first fence. **Don't Push It** jumped the first well, jumped the second well, then he came to the third fence. The big ditch, probably the most difficult fence on the course, coming, as it does, so early in the race. He sailed over it. He was taking to these fences, he was enjoying himself over them. He could just run a big race here, I thought. He has every chance of getting around at the very least.

I heard the cheers from the grandstand as we passed the winning post for the first time and headed out again. Just one more lap, and my feeling of, 'God, I'm enjoying this,' turned to, 'you know what? We could win this.'

There were only two or three horses that were travelling well in front of me. Barry was going well on **Big Fella Thanks**, Denis O'Regan was going well on **Black Apalachi**. But he had been forcing a strong pace with **Conna Castle** for a while. Daryl Jacob was going well on **Maljimar**, but I was not certain that he would stay. Of course, there was a long way to go. There would be other horses staying on from behind, but there could not have been many others with a chance.

Over the Foinavon fence, towards the Canal Turn, I angled him out so that he could jump it at an angle. And he flew it, just as he had done on the first circuit. **Maljimar** started to drop away, and suddenly there were only four of us. Of the four, **Big Fella Thanks** was the one that I feared most. Barry seemed to have plenty left in the tank, and **Black Apalachi** and **Hello Bud** had been up there with the strong pace from the start.

At the second fence down the side of the course, **Hello Bud** jumped in front of us and we made a mistake. It halted our momentum a bit. But he still had plenty of energy left, and we were still upright. Going to the second-last, I gave him a squeeze and asked him to make ground up on the outside of the other three. He picked up nicely. We landed over the second-last alongside **Black Apalachi**, almost in front. I could see Barry wilting. I knew my fellow would keep going, but I was still thinking, 'not yet, it's a long way from the last fence to the line.' Down to the last, and I was just looking for a stride. Got one. I asked him to pick up and he did, jumping the fence perfectly.

We got to the Elbow and **Black Apalachi** was still there on my inside. Dogged as you like. He just would not go away. When the rail appeared, I moved my horse in towards it. I did not want to cut the nose off **Black Apalachi**. I did not want to risk a stewards' inquiry. But I did want to get the rail in front of him, to give him a reason to down tools. Just sicken him a little. I got onto the rail in front of **Black Apalachi**, and just sat down and drove for the line. I had a little look under my right shoulder and could see **Black Apalachi** getting further behind me. I looked ahead and could see the winning line getting closer. I wanted to scream. I thought, 'is this really happening? Could this be it? After all these years? Is this really the Grand National? Is this dreamland?'

Valerie Mulcahy

Valerie Mulcahy played at senior level Gaelic football for Cork, winning ten All-Ireland medals and nine Ladies' National Football League titles between 2005 and 2015. She was also an All Star on six occasions. As a women's association football player, she represented Ireland at the 2003 Summer Universiade and played for Cork City in the Women's National League. In 2015 Mulcahy helped launch the Women's Gaelic Players' Association.

In this extract from the book *At the End of the Day*, edited by Paul Byrnes, Mulcahy reflects on her decision to finally retire from football.

At the End of the Day

If sport is an addiction, then retiring is like coming down off something. You no longer have that structure in your life. There is no more training. No more travelling. And you are no longer competing at the highest level. It takes a bit of adjusting and time to get used to retirement. Many players who retired before me said they still miss the big day. That buzz. And how much they would look forward to playing and competing. When that goes, it is very hard to replace it.

There was a moment in 2015 when I decided that was it. It was time to retire. I had been considering for a long time how and when I should retire. And I had been appreciating much more than usual all the success we had experienced as a team, over the years. I had just got married and my mother-in-law was terminally ill. Life outside football was getting bigger and fuller for me. Others were becoming more reliant on me. So spending so much time on football was getting harder to justify to myself.

At the start of each season, every player thinks about what is ahead of them and all that is involved in the year. There is the travelling, the training and all those weekends away. You think about everything and everyone you will miss. It is a massive commitment. It is not easy to balance everything including work, life, and now marriage for me.

My wife had followed me to every end of the country and had supported me in every way possible since I had known her. Now her mother was sick. I wanted to be available to support her as she had supported me.

I really enjoyed my final game in Croke Park. I knew I was about to retire and that it would be my last game. I just savoured the moment. I was not looking back or looking forward. I was living in the present.

It was such a great feeling. I was also leaving at a great time. We had won another All Ireland title with an incredible team and I played my part.

I was very content with my decision to retire. For 15 years, I had prioritised ladies' football over everything else in my life. I look back on my career with so many wonderful memories. There were so many great days and magical moments.

One of those days, my most treasured day in my career, has to be the 2014 All-Ireland Senior Football Final against Dublin. We were being well beaten and for the first time ever, it looked like we would be beaten in Croke Park. Thankfully, we managed to produce a very memorable comeback that I will be proud of for the rest of my life. That moment still brings a smile to my face every time I think about it.

Winning is an amazing feeling. I feel there are two types of winning. There is winning when you are the underdog and that incredible feeling of victory and jubilation at the final whistle. And then there is winning when you are expected to win and it has become the norm and just the pure relief of defending your position. You are just so happy you have managed not to lose.

Losing can be a complete shock and it can hurt, really hurt. We lost the 2010 All-Ireland Senior Football Quarter Final to Tyrone after being well up at half time. The reality that we had lost was shocking. I did not cry that day. In a funny way, I always knew that day would come. It is a horrible place to be. It was so disappointing and I didn't know what to do for the rest of the season.

Thankfully, I've been very lucky as a player. The great team I have played with. I haven't experienced loss too often, for which I am so grateful to my coach and my team mates.

Looking back on my career, I will always be very grateful for everything I have had. We came from such lows. Having five players at training for a championship match. Getting thrashed by Waterford and Kerry in the Munster football championship. We went from that to achieving greatness in the sport.

It far exceeded anything I ever imagined, hoped for or dreamed of. I had a dream of winning one All Ireland. We won ten with an unbelievable team. It was amazing to be part of something great. We made history. We changed the record books and helped increase the profile of ladies' football in the process.

Summer will never be the same without my Cork jersey and football boots, as I know I will never have those special moments again. So, it is hugely important for sports people to enjoy every moment, particularly as you get older, and your career is coming to an end. My advice to players now is to be present. Enjoy the moment for what it is and savour the journey.

Barry McGuigan

Barry McGuigan is a former champion boxer. In June 1985, he beat Eusebio Pedroza to become the featherweight champion of the world. In the following extract from his autobiography, *Cyclone*, he remembers this iconic fight. It was an epic battle that lasted a full 15 rounds, and it remains one of sport's greatest moments. He currently enjoys a successful career as a sports commentator, writer and motivational speaker. He is president and founder of the Professional Boxing Association and is a boxing promoter and trainer. He has coached his youngest son Shane to national titles in England and Ireland.

Cyclone

I had never set foot in Loftus Road before the Pedroza fight. In fact, I never went back until 2005 when I was filming a programme for Sky Sports, to mark the twentieth anniversary of my winning the world title. I did not recognise anything as we were driving in, until we got to the entrance and I saw this flash of blue on the outside of the building. Then it all came back to me. Suddenly I could remember it all as though it was yesterday. Pulling up. Walking straight through and down to where the dressing rooms were. I was in the home dressing room that night, Pedroza the away.

The fight was a 27,000-seat sell-out. By the time we got to Loftus Road that evening, driving from my central London hotel in the Team McGuigan bus, most of the fans were already inside. Earlier in the day, we had used the bus as a decoy. Driving to the weigh-in in a separate car to avoid the crush of fans. That evening, with fight time approaching, the streets were quieter. I still recall seeing a fair few supporters milling about and making their way to the stadium. What I really remember about arriving was the noise. You could hear this buzz from inside the ground and that really pumped me up. As we waited in the dressing room it built and built and got louder and louder. Because the fight was on television, everyone knew exactly what time I would be coming out. The closer it got to my entrance time, the more the expectation and the atmosphere grew.

While all that was going on, Pedroza's people were still trying to pull their tricks. We had sent my brother Dermot into Pedroza's dressing room to watch him bandage up. Pedroza's manager, Santiago Del Rio, came in to watch me. Dermot didn't tell me until afterwards, but Pedroza played it cool in front of him. He looked huge, Dermot told me later. Big muscular arms and completely relaxed. He was chatting away in Spanish and looking at my brother and smiling, confident as you like. Dermot watched the bandages being wrapped and told them that they were fine.

Del Rio came in to watch my hands being bandaged. He was determined to do what he could to wind me up. What you do with the hands is you wrap your surgical bandage back and forth over your knuckles to build a pad. The knuckles are the first point of impact. It is where the energy and trauma are absorbed. Therefore you try to protect them by creating a pad with the bandage. Del Rio was watching all this carefully, same as we had always done them. He said, 'What is this? Let me see that.' So we showed him and he shook his head: 'Too much, too much.' We took it all off and had to start again. He was still complaining and I lost it.

I swore at him and said, 'For fuck's sake.' Del Rio looked at me and said, 'Mmm ... OK, OK, right.' He left because he had achieved what he'd come to do. To get me going. Del Rio had succeeded in that, and did not even stay to watch us do the other hand.

I was annoyed, really annoyed, but I'm not sure that his plan really worked. The incident just served to pump me up even more. Not that I needed it. I was already on a high, but after that I was really revved up. I gloved up and the noise outside was rising to a crescendo. All you could hear was this thump-thump-thump because the dressing room was right underneath the stand. Every time the door opened, this wave of sound from outside came crashing in.

Someone with a set of headphones on came in and said, 'Right, let's go.' Because I was the challenger, I would be brought out first. We had the Rocky theme playing over the PA (public address) system. Everyone has their music now but I swear, honest to God, that we were the first to do that. The noise was so loud, so deafening, however, that you could hardly hear the music above the crowd.

We came out and were supposed to turn left and walk along the side of the football pitch by these metal barriers. Then someone out front took the decision not to go on our original route. We were not going to go left because there were all these people, thousands of them, standing in the way. There was no way we were going to move them all back without causing a scene. So we just got the barrier lifted up and out, and went straight for the ring. We had to move around some seats, saying 'Excuse me, excuse me' to people. We walked to the ring like that. All in all, it took us twelve minutes to get from the dressing room to the ring. It was so slow and took so long that the American TV station broadcasting the fight had to keep going to ad breaks.

I could see how large the stadium was, and how big the crowd was too. Everyone was getting excited. They were all up and cheering, but I just kept my head down as well as I could. I didn't want to make a big fuss. I just wanted to get to the ring. I had this guy Vince McCormack, who used to walk with me through the crowd before the fight, with Sean McGivern, Barney Eastwood and all my team. We had this routine where we would recite a little prayer as we walked to the ring. It was called 'Angel of God': 'Ever this day be at my side, to light and guard, to rule and guide.' It was as much routine as anything. Something to focus your mind with everything else going on. Such was the noise and the madness that night, you could not hear yourself think. Let alone hear the words. So I just repeated them to myself, over and over, as we made our way towards the ring.

I climbed through the ropes to more cheers, and Pedroza came in. There was no interruption with him from the fans. He just walked straight through. I was in the ring and moving around and then, within a few minutes, he got in on the other side of the ring.

You couldn't make this up, but then a little guy dressed up as a leprechaun appeared. That was Barney Eastwood's idea. He had heard and seen how Sean O'Grady in the States had a dwarf dressed up as a leprechaun in the ring before the fight. Throwing his magic dust to bring good luck. People from Panama are meant to be wary of old folk tales and Barney thought it might spook Pedroza. As if. But he got this act in, had him skipping and tumbling about the ring. I was not looking at Pedroza, but glanced across the ring as this was going on, and remember catching sight of his hooded figure.

My father got up to sing 'Danny Boy'. That was a big deal for me, that he was there singing. Yet at the same time as he was singing and everyone was joining in, I had to separate myself from it, and make sure that I didn't get caught up in the emotion of it all. As much as I wanted to listen to him, I had to let it wash over me and focus on the fight. While Dad was singing, Dermot shouted that Pedroza was staring at me, giving me this dead-eyed stare. He was trying to psych me out but, actually, it was the perfect distraction from the song. I gave him the stare back, to let him know I was ready for him and meant business.

I was there to do a job. I had to have my head right for potentially fifteen flat-out rounds. I had to be ready to push Pedroza back and bully him. To take control and win the fight. That was my objective. Nothing could distract me from that. Not even the sound of my father leading the 27,000 fans singing this emotionally charged song. I figured I could always listen to that later, and I did, many times. Especially after my dad had passed away, I would listen to him singing and it always made me cry. But all that was for later, much later. The ring was clearing. The noise was rising. The waiting was over. In front of 27,000 fight fans, 20 million watching at home and God knows how many abroad. There was just me, Pedroza and 15 rounds to decide the featherweight championship of the world.

Cora Staunton

Since her inter-county Gaelic football debut at the age of thirteen, Cora Staunton has gone on to win four senior All-Ireland Championships with Mayo, featuring in 67 Championship games over 23 seasons. She has led her club team, Carnacon, to six All-Ireland titles and has won 11 All-Star Awards. In 2017, Cora became the first international player signing in the Australian Women's Football League.

In the following extract from her bestselling autobiography, *Game Changer*, she recalls her involvement in the the 1999 All-Ireland Senior Ladies' Football Championship Final.

Game Changer

The buzz around Mayo in 1999 was mighty. There was bunting nearly hanging off cattle. Every old fella with a cap was reading about us from a bar stool. This level of support was only ever rolled out when the Mayo men got to Croke Park. They had returned empty-handed, twice out of the last three seasons, so the fuss was about us redeeming ourselves as a county more than anything.

We were a glimmer of hope for people. And that was when it dawned on me what playing for Mayo was really about. We were giving people something to believe in. Before, I was just a teenager putting a green and red jersey on over my head, hoping I played well. Now, I knew the meaning of those colours, and how deep the dye ran. I realised that I was representing something much bigger than myself.

Some say that brings added pressure, but I only ever saw it as a privilege. And, whether it was Mayo or Carnacon, the passion always boiled at the same temperature for me. Club is your bread and butter. It is who you are. Yet that is balanced by the honour of playing for your county. So when the reality of what it meant to run out in Croke Park wearing a Mayo jersey hit, the day could not come fast enough.

Seven days out, we trained in Ballinrobe. It was the last time any of us had a chance to impress the coach, Finbar Egan. In those A versus B games, someone was always on the edge of rejection or a spot on the team. Their year could amount to nothing, or it could amount to something. For 50 minutes, we went 100 miles an hour. No one came up for air. I was on the dugout side of the pitch, tucked into the corner, when a ball came in low. Claire Egan had the same idea, and as we collided, I heard a loud cracking sound followed by a sharp shooting pain in my shoulder. Immediately I knew it did not feel right. I had snapped my collarbone. My shoulder slumped, with nothing there to hold its frame in place. Claire looked on in shock as the lads ran over.

The thought of missing the All-Ireland final had not yet entered my head. That was until I caught sight of a few of the girls. Their faces said it all. It was bad. In my head I started to panic and cry. My cousin, Maria Staunton, and Niamh Lally drove me to Accident and Emergency (A&E) in Mayo General Hospital. I sat in the back seat, and I remember watching them, the tears running down their cheeks. When we got there, Dad and Kathleen were already waiting for me. The last time we were all there together was the night Mam died. The last fourteen months of football with Mayo had distracted us all. Getting to the All-Ireland senior final was a new beginning for all of us. The team was winning. Parents had gotten to know one another, and Dad enjoyed getting out to games. Going back to play with Mayo after Mam passed away had also made me cop on. I had realised it was just Dad now and I did not want to cause him any more trouble. Yet there I was landed in A&E.

When we got home, I locked myself in my bedroom. I did not come out for hours. I was numb. It was almost how I felt when Mam died. Not that I cried a lot. I just sat there trying desperately to make sense of it all.

Obviously, the preparations continued at full pelt, but I felt a little isolated from the group. It had nothing to do with the girls. I just didn't feel like I was in the thick of it. I was on the outside looking in. I was the missing link in our 'Up and Downs' and that was difficult for me.

Just as we had done for the All-Ireland semi-final, we stayed the night before in Maynooth University in Kildare. Maria and I roomed together, and just before we headed to the Glenroyal Hotel for dinner there was a knock at the door. It was Finbar. He sat down in a chair in the corner of the room as if he was just coming in for a chat, and then out of the blue he told me that I was starting on Sunday. They would leave me on for the first 30 seconds, and then I would make way. I could not believe it, but he was deadly serious. He had even spoken to Michael Ryan, the Waterford coach, to make sure that his players knew not to nail me in the opening minute. Hearing that news took my mind off everything. I was back on the inside, and I would finally get to wear the green and red of Mayo in Croke Park.

Looking back, I'm sure Finbar was only doing it to help me. In the previous months, we had built up a bit of a relationship and he had learned what I had gone through at home with Mam. By letting me start, it was his way of easing some of the pain for me. On the day of the final, 3 October 1999, there were 15,101 people in Croke Park.

It was a long road from Carnacon's home pitch, Clogher, to Croke Park, and I was so grateful to get to start. As I followed the Artane Band around the pitch in the pre-match team march, my right arm dangled limply. I did not want to wear a sling because that would show weakness. When the whistle blew, I cherished what turned out to be the next 47 seconds at corner-forward. I took in the rush. I took in the Hill and the sound of the crowd, before Finbar called me and sent in Orla Casby to the half-forward line. She already had the slip of paper ready to pull from her sock and when she came on, everyone knew to rotate in the forward line. As a result, Michael Ryan spent the next five minutes reshuffling his own crew.

It was horrible to have to watch the game from the bench. I felt helpless, and every now and then, I snuck out of the dugout and wandered down to the sideline. I had to get closer or I would have lost my mind. We started slowly when it came to getting scores. Once settled, we got in a rhythm. Points from Diane O'Hora, Sabrina Bailey and Christina Heffernan saw us lead by a point at half-time (0–5 to 0–4).

In the dressing room, we did not think we had it won, but we believed in ourselves. Less than a minute after the restart, Diane and Christina both fired over frees, and Imelda Mullarkey, our corner-back, added another point from play. We were in the zone. But Waterford were going for a possible sixth title in a decade, and Michael Ryan instructed his players to throw everything at us in the final quarter. They did, but we managed to keep them three points adrift.

In the last ten minutes the 'Up and Downs' kicked in, and Waterford started to cramp. It was happening, and we were outrunning them, with Sinéad Costello picking off a vital point to widen the gap to four points (0–12 to 0–8). For the first time ever the countdown clock was used in Croker, and as the seconds ticked, the crowd lifted. A section of fans behind our dugout started to sing 'We Are The Champions' before the whistle went. Suddenly, we had done it.

As the substitutes ran on, a reporter grabbed me for a word. And let me just say I made a fool of myself. 'We have done what the Mayo men couldn't do!' I shouted down the camera lens. It was my first interview on television, and it was a fierce stupid thing to say. It is one of a few regrets I have in my career, because I should have known how hard it was to bloody win one.

The lads had given it everything and more, and in my moment of madness, I forgot that. Thankfully there was not a big deal made out of it in the aftermath. I feared that there would be, but Mayo people understood the emotion that was involved and all they were interested in was celebrating with us.

That night we attended the Ladies' Gaelic Football Association's victory function at Jurys Hotel in Ballsbridge. We enjoyed the celebrations. The next morning, when I lifted my head off the pillow, a smile shot across my face. I know I only featured for all of 47 seconds, but I had put in as many 'Up and Downs' as the rest of them. That is what made us, the savagery of those sprints. If you asked me, 'Would you do it all over again?' Absolutely. Vomit and all!

The homecoming west to Mayo was one of the best nights of my life. We crossed over the Galway border into Shrule on Monday evening. Our bus driver, Eoin Cronin, probably put down the toughest shift of his life. The majority of us crashed in Yvonne Byrne's three-bedroom house in Ballyhaunis. There was not a bit of flooring to be seen.

Yvonne – or Crazy as she was known to us – was a solid centre-back who played her club football with Hollymount. Her mother, Margaret, was the County Board treasurer and she was only delighted with life that we had gone and won the Brendan Martin Cup. She loved the banter and minding us all too. By the time I surfaced the next day, she already had our jerseys washed and ironed. Her sister-in-law, Joan, had even come over to help make us all a bite to eat.

Fed and watered, we took off again, but first, a few of us popped around to one of Crazy's neighbours with the cup. Katie Johnson was 100 years old and a proud Mayo woman. She had seen a lot in her lifetime. Two world wars and a civil war. But she had never seen the Brendan Martin Cup coming back to her home county. Seeing the glint in her eye made me realise just how rare it was to win, and the joy it brought to others. Mam was not there to witness it, and I missed out on that. But all I needed to do was look down and read the crest on the Mayo jersey to know that she was there. It read: Dia is Muire Linn. God, and Mary, be with us. I think she was.

Niall Quinn

As a player Niall Quinn was a striker who played top flight football for Arsenal, Manchester City and Sunderland football clubs. Quinn also received 92 caps for the Republic of Ireland national football team, scoring 21 times. This makes him Ireland's second highest goal scorer of all time. He also appeared with the Irish team at the UEFA (Union of European Football Associations) European Football Championship of 1988 and two FIFA (Fédération Internationale de Football Association) World Cups in 1990 and 2002. He went on to become chairman and manager of Sunderland Football Club, before leaving the club in 2012.

In this extract from his *World Cup Diary*, an Open Door book published in 2004, he writes about the World Cup match between Ireland and Spain in 2002.

Republic of Ireland versus Spain

17 June 2002

I have no regrets.

It is a cruel way to go out of the World Cup, of course. But something exciting has taken shape here. I may be coming to the end, but this Ireland team is going to be in big tournaments for many years to come. I have no doubt about that. The next eight years, I believe, are going to be a golden era for Irish soccer.

That is what this tournament has shown. I am not going home lamenting missed penalty kicks. I am delighted with myself that I had some role to play. I thought I had seen it all with Ireland. I thought I had seen it all in my career. But this World Cup was new territory. Unbelievable. I have loved every minute. I just wish I were a few years younger.

I found it very emotional at the end, walking off knowing that my international career was over. But it is not anything I want to dwell on. You just take your leave and walk away.

What a way to sign off! It could have been a damp, cold night playing away to Russia, getting dumped out of some qualifying tournament. But this was unforgettable. An incredible few weeks that we all travelled through as one. Fans, players and staff. Maybe it is because I am older, I do not know. But this will bring me far happier memories than anything I have done before.

I was due to take the sixth penalty. I honestly felt that Shay was going to save from Mendieta. I was getting ready for the kick. I just wanted one more kick in an Ireland shirt. But it was not to be.

I was actually quite confident I would score. When they missed their fourth, and their second in a row, I thought we had them. And what a scruffy penalty it was that claimed the victory. I thought Tony Cascarino took the biscuit for scruffy penalties. A divot (a square of turf or sod) hit the net the same time as the ball, when Tony took his famous kick in Genoa. But

Mendieta's was every bit as poor. It was probably the worst penalty he has ever taken. That's life.

I know the lads who missed are hurting. But they have to look at their ages and assess fairly what they have achieved in this tournament. We have had incredible highs out here, and an incredible low at the end. That is what you need to go through.

These guys became real men, real Irish heroes in this World Cup. Especially the five penalty takers. Six actually, because Ian Harte is a hero in my eyes for being brave enough to take one in normal time.

These guys have to be positive now. I think the days of Ireland being happy just to qualify for a tournament are over. We are going to have far more serious intentions from now on.

Funny how informal everything becomes in the middle of the cauldron. We had a fair idea from training who wanted to take the penalties and in what order. Mark Kinsella and myself were deciding who would go in sixth and seventh. I said I would go sixth. Mark laughed back, reminding me that he had actually taken one when Charlton beat us at Wembley.

There was no sense of panic, no terror. Penalties, effectively, come down to luck. We didn't get it. But no one should feel in any way ashamed.

What do you say to the poor guys who missed? Well, you remind them of perspective. When Mattie Holland came back to the centre circle he was devastated. But, let's be honest, he has become an Irish legend with what he has done over the last few weeks. He had the disappointment of relegation with Ipswich this season, but he has had a wonderful World Cup. Yes, it was a low way to finish. But I just said to him, 'Look, you are a world-class player now. How bad is that? Why be down on yourself?'

Poor Kevin Kilbane was beside himself. He had a magnificent game last night. He showed for the ball from the first whistle. Things did not fall kindly for him. Between the penalty miss, and the skewed rebound after Harry's effort was parried (defended) by Casillas. But he was fantastic. Kevin Kilbane has set the standard for himself now. He has got another 40 caps in him, and hopefully most of them will come at big tournaments.

Someone said afterwards there is a big homecoming planned for us in Dublin. The people have always amazed me, but never more than on this trip. I don't know whether it is because we have been so far away from home or because of everything that went on in the build-up. But the power of what happened here has been frightening. If the players get a homecoming, I will be telling them to save every memory, as it is precious.

I did not do that in 1990, and I feel guilty for it. I was younger and, in many ways, let the moment slip by. Well I will not be letting this one slip, no matter who turns up to meet us.

We had two or three retirement parties last night. Some guys were down afterwards, others not so bad. The important thing is that people remind these players how good they are, how good they have been and how good they can now become.

Duffer? For 120 minutes, he was absolutely fantastic. Breath-taking. He is one fella I'll be glad to tell my grandchildren that I played with.

Robbie? He scored three World Cup goals. Four actually, if you include his second penalty. He grew up so much over here. People still talk about Robbie in slightly negative terms. About it not happening for him at Inter, and Dave O'Leary not playing him that much now at Leeds. But he is going back now with his chest out. Watch Robbie Keane, I say. Because he is going to be sensational. He has been a star.

And, out here, I would say he was in good company.

Bonnar Ó Loingsigh

Abood Al Jumaili - also known as Bonnar Ó Loingsigh - came to Ireland from Iraq in 2008 with his family. He currently plays hurling for the Ballinteer Saint Johns club, and is an AIG (American International Group) - Dublin GAA (Gaelic Athletic Association) Diversity and Inclusion ambassador. The following piece is a speech Ó Loingsigh made at the celebration of the Muslim festival of Eid at Croke Park in 2020. He reflects on coming to Ireland as a child and getting involved in GAA.

Speech made at Eid celebration at Croke Park

31 July 2020

I greet you all with the Islamic greeting of peace, **As-salaam alaikum**. Peace be with you all. **Dia dhuit.**

I am **Abdullah Al Jumaili**, also known as Bonnar Ó Loingsigh. I am originally from Iraq, Baghdad, and I can proudly say with chest wide open that I am Irish too.

I moved to Ireland in 2008. I started primary school straight away. I did not have a word of English, apart from saying 'Hi'. I remember just sitting in class and writing what the teacher was writing on the board, even though I did not understand it.

One day I was walking around my primary school at lunch time, and I heard some students talking about hurling. I had no clue what it was. At half two, it was home time. I was leaving my class and I saw some boys were going off to train. It caught my eye. I had a quick look but forgot about it soon enough. I did not really take too much notice of them.

In a couple of weeks' time, two teachers came up to me and asked me if I would be interested in trying out for the school hurling team. 'Sure why not?' I said. So I started training. It did not really appeal to me at the time. I was frustrated at that moment. I could not even hold the hurl properly. I woke up the next day, picked up the hurl and started trying to at least lift the ball. I kept at it and kept at it and kept at it, until eventually I lifted the ball. I realised that I had fallen in love with, in my view and as many will agree, the best game on earth. I am sure many will agree.

From there my hurling career started and has grown into an obsession with hurling, which is getting stronger with every puck of the sliotar (hurling ball). It started to become so important to me that I went out every day to practise – no matter if it was lashing rain, hailstones, snow or even thunder. No matter what it was, you could count on me to be either at my back garden or my local pitch, getting my accuracy in touch up. I play hurling with my club, Ballinteer Saint John's. I also play hurling for my college Dublin Institute of Technology, now Technological University (TU) Dublin City Campus, where I also study Law. I am going into my final year now.

It was tough starting off hurling as a Muslim here as I did not really speak the language. I did not understand the people nor did I even know the system. But now Ireland is my home. And although I have had some daydreams of living in Muslim society, I could not see myself leaving my home land. I feel comfortable and truly at home here, where I understand the people, the culture and the system. And I also feel care and responsibility towards my Irish people. I would like to thank the Irish Muslim Peace and Integration Council for providing a platform to Irish Muslims to celebrate their dual identity of being Irish and being Muslim. And inspiring us with the vision of bridging communities and building peace. I also would like to thank the GAA and Croke Park especially for making this wonderful event happen with the Irish Muslim Peace and Integration Council.

To everyone else here, no matter where you are in the country, no matter where you are from, try GAA, where we all belong. **Eid Mubarak, go raibh maith agat, slán agat.**

Glossary of words

Arabic words

Arabic word	Pronounced	Meaning
EID celebration	i-eed	EID is a celebration to mark the ending of the month-long fast of Ramadan. Ramadan is a month when Muslims across the world fast from dawn to dusk.
As-salaam alaikum	Ass-alam a-lay-kum	This means 'peace be upon you'.
Eid Mubarak	Eed mu-ba-rack	This means 'Blessed feast or festival'.

Irish words

Irish word	Pronounced	Meaning
Dia dhuit	dee-ah gwit	It is a greeting in the Irish language and means hello. The literal translation is 'God be with you.'
Go raibh maith agat	guh rev mah agut	It means thank you. The literal translation is 'may you have goodness.'
Slán agat	slawn a-gut	It means goodbye. The literal translation is 'have safety'.

Rosemary Smith

Rosemary Smith is a rally driver from Dublin. Her father taught her to drive at the age of 11 in a field in Tallaght. Leaving school at 15, Rosemary trained as a dress designer and model and opened a dressmaking company. Rosemary was asked to navigate for a friend in a rally but soon took over the driving. Rosemary was the first and only woman driver to win the Tulip Rally outright, beating all the male drivers to the finish. In the following extract from her book *Driven*, she recalls the epic 1970 World Cup London to Mexico Rally.

Rosemary is passionate about road safety and opened the Rosemary Smith School of Motoring in 1999 where she teaches young people to drive. In 2017, at 80 years of age, she became the oldest person to drive a Renault Sports Formula One team car.

South of the Border

The London to Sydney Marathon was a success because I finished, when 42 other competitors had fallen by the wayside. It was well known in the industry that I had overcome many obstacles along the way. No doubt it was because of this, that British Leyland got the notion that I was a good bet for the mammoth 1970 World Cup London to Mexico Rally.

Yet again I was being used for publicity purposes. British Leyland needed all the exposure it could get because the Austin Maxi was a new car on the market. I do not think they really cared if I got there or not, as long as I flashed my legs and looked pretty. We posed before the orange and white candy striped Austin, in full-length white coats and white leather boots. The outfits were amazing but totally impractical for rallying. Our rally outfits were a blue jacket and red trousers. Alice Watson and Ginette de Rolland were my co-drivers.

The team had done everything they could to make the car, which was a new and untried model, ready for the long trip.... Nobody could know how the Maxi would respond to the long drive. Or if it would get beyond Lisbon.... Alice, Ginette and I climbed into our orange and white striped Austin Maxi on 19 April 1970. We knew that the epic drive to Mexico would end on 22 May, if we managed to get that far. Our Maxi was 1475cc, much smaller than the rest of the team. They had cars with 1800cc engines.

At the beginning, 98 cars, from 22 countries, started out from Wembley. Minis and Fords from Britain. Moskviches from Russia. A Toyota from Japan. A Beach Buggy. A Wagoneer Jeep from the U.S. (United States) and even two Rolls-Royces. The course covered over 16,000 miles (25,700 km) – 5,000 miles through Europe and the rest through South and Central America.

The drive through Europe was not difficult, but the dust and roads in Yugoslavia were challenging. During the seven days of the European leg there was only one scheduled overnight stop in Monza, Italy. We took it in turns to sleep. By the time we reached Lisbon, only 71 cars were left out of the 96 starters.

We had to fly from Lisbon Airport to Rio de Janeiro. The media were all over us when we got there. As I stepped into the hotel swimming pool in my white bikini, the flashbulbs were popping. No doubt that was what British Leyland was hoping for. I didn't let them down!

On Friday, 8 May, at the start of our journey through Brazil, we departed Rio to a flag-waving crowd, loud music and excited pressmen. BMC's (British Motor Company's) competition manager was concerned about the floods forecast. When the rain came we had to contend with hailstones the size of golf balls crashing down on us. Some of the drivers pulled over and took shelter under the trees. I saw no need for that and just kept going. Crossing the narrow wooden bridges, which appeared out of nowhere, was challenging. There was no other way round.

After 40 hours of non-stop driving we reached Montevideo. We were one of only 52 cars that had got that far. After a much-needed night's sleep, we boarded the car ferry, for the three-hour journey across the River Plate to Buenos Aires.

We drove through the amazing landscape of Central America with barely time to register what was around us. With my dress-designing hat on, I could not miss the women. Their clothes were like nothing I had ever seen before. Everywhere in the mountains you would see them in beautiful garments of vibrant red, orange, blue and green. They always wore hats. Wonderful, wide brimmed hats.

There were only two things that went wrong with the car. The cassette player and the fan belt. On a very bumpy road, the cassette player started of its own accord and suddenly Elvis was singing 'All Shook Up'. I nearly jumped out of my skin; Alice managed to turn him off before I got too excited. But that was only a minor thing. The fan belt was a little more serious.

When I saw the temperature gauge going up and up I knew we were in trouble. We stopped at the top of the mountain and waited for someone to come along. As luck would have it, Tony Fall, who was driving a Ford Escort, came to our rescue. Jimmy Greaves was his co-driver and was really only there for publicity purposes. As it turned out he was a very good driver as well as a footballer.

Tony Fall put the fan belt on and we were ready to go. We looked around for Alice, but she was nowhere to be seen. When we found her, she looked like a little green shrub. She was covered in cactus flies bigger than grasshoppers. They were sucking her arms, face and any bit of skin that was exposed. We tried to hit them off, but they must have liked her Scottish blood and would not move. The only thing I could think of was to take the fire extinguisher and spray her all over. I was told afterwards they could have given her awful burns, but it worked.

The horrible insects fell off and we got her into the car and drove off.

As the day wore on, Alice blew up like a balloon and was covered in what looked like a very bad case of measles. When we got to the control stop, I had to cut off her clothes, her watch and everything. We fed her glucose drinks just to keep her going. When we arrived at La Paz I knew we had to get her to hospital because she was drifting in and out of consciousness. The stewards at the top of the mountain were insisting that I couldn't go down as it was past midnight. It was a very narrow pass, with cliffs on one side and a deep drop on the other. We were told that trucks were due to be coming up during the night.

I crashed a barrier that the stewards had put across the road. I was sure Alice would die if we did not get help for her. Halfway down the pass, we could see trucks approaching. Ginette put her foot on the horn and kept it there. Someone must have telephoned and said some mad women are coming down the mountain, keep out of their way. I didn't care if the car was damaged, I just wanted to get Alice to the hospital.

We had an overnight in La Paz. Ginette and I resigned ourselves to the fact that this was the end for us and the rally. If you started with a team of three, all of you had to finish. That was the rule. Later the next day there was a knock on the door. There she was, with her feet barely touching the ground, as two male nurses held her up. Alice knew if she didn't come with us we were out of the running.

Alice still wasn't well, but at least we had medication for her and an assurance from the doctor that she would recover. And so we left La Paz on Sunday 17 May, en route to Lima in Peru. The going was rough. Nine of the 39 cars that left La Paz never made it to Lima.

26 cars got as far as the port at Buenaventura to board the MS Verdi for the two-day trip to Central America. We sailed up the Pacific coast of Colombia and then through the Panama Canal on 23 May.

At the border between Costa Rica and Nicaragua the national cleansing department sprayed all the cars with disinfectant. We were well and truly fumigated. The smell in the car was awful. In the early hours of the morning, dark except for our headlights glaring we came round a bend to find huge rocks blocking our way. Half joking, I said to Alice and Ginette, 'You had better get out and move them out of the way.' That was when we heard the sound of horses' hooves. Five men on horseback galloped towards us with big sombreros and handkerchiefs tied around their faces. When they realised we were women, they started to question us.

'What are you doing?' We explained we were on a rally. 'Where are you going?' Mexico City, we told them.

'What have you got in the car?' We told them nothing but a few clothes. Then they proceeded to lecture us, telling us that we should not be out in the middle of the night. How very dangerous it was. They cautioned us to be careful. They acted like true gentlemen, rolled the rocks out of the way and left us to it.

We went on. The long hours of driving were starting to take their toll on me.

'How much longer, Alice?' I asked.

'Soon, soon,' she said, looking at the road book, and just then we came over the brow of the hill. All the lights were spread out below us. It was Fortin, a night halt 300 miles from Mexico City. We had made it to the last checkpoint....

There were 98 contestants in all and only 23 arrived at the Estadio Azteca in Mexico. Five female crews left Wembley that day, two made it to the finish. We were one of them. Gaining tenth place overall and beating 11 other all-male teams....

The cars were washed and polished. We had a police escort into the stadium. Suddenly, the rain came down in torrents. All the spectators, who might have enjoyed the spectacle of 23 cars, in various states of disrepair, speeding along, disappeared. As we approached the Estadio

Azteca the rain eased off and the cars got in line. The first three headed by Hannu Mikkola and Gunnar Palm, the winners, were to enter first. Because we had won the Ladies' Section we were to go in after them.

It was pure determination that we finished that rally. Well, that and my outstanding driving skills, of course!

Henry Shefflin

Henry Shefflin is often regarded as one of the greatest hurlers in the history of the sport. He has more All-Stars, Hurler of the Year awards and All-Ireland medals than any other hurler. He retired from playing inter-county hurling in 2015, and is the current manager of the Galway Senior hurling team.

In the following extract from his autobiography, he recalls the 2014 All-Ireland Senior Hurling Championship Final.

The Dream

There is no point pretending that my tenth All-Ireland medal came in the fashion I would have chosen. I wanted to be starting.

It was not what I dreamed of. All the way through the season, I put a fierce amount of pressure on myself. But I can honestly say that the vibe in the Kilkenny squad, the chemistry between young and old, was as good as I could ever remember it. So, yes, I became a bit-player (someone who plays a small role in something) in the end. But I could still embrace that special sense of a group working to be the absolute best that it could be.

No question, the personal unease never fully lifted. For the first run of the 2014 final – which was a draw game – I was called down out of the stand three times before being eventually put on. Aiden 'Taggy' Fogarty had been the first forward sub (substitute) in after maybe 50 minutes and, shortly afterwards, I got the signal to get ready.

I spent about five minutes warming up on the line before James McGarry told me to go back up into the stand. Soon after, another signal to get ready and – this time – maybe ten minutes spent stretching and waiting. Brian Cody was just a few yards away, totally consumed by the game.

What could I do? Tap him on the shoulder? Start tugging at his sleeve like I used do as a child with Joe Dunphy in Ballyhale National School?

You feel as if the whole stadium is looking at you when, in reality, everyone is completely spellbound by an extraordinary game. Maybe the only people who could see me were family.

In retrospect, I could have no issue with Brian. The game was crazy. Just charging along independent of logic, pattern or form-line. In those circumstances, a manager is only human if he keeps changing his mind. A forward might be having a nightmare, but just one little touch wins a stay of execution.

'Jesus, we can't take him off, he is coming into this …'

But there are 82,000 people in Croke Park, and you are standing there, aware only of your own situation. I felt almost like an old man in the end, flicking out his leg just for want of something better to do. Eventually, I made the decision myself, turned away and climbed back up into the stand.

When the third call came, there was probably a bit of impatience visible in my body language. I went down and put my helmet straight on, as if to say, 'Am I going on or not?'

Finally, with three minutes to go, I was sent in to full-forward with instructions to try to hold the ball up there. We were three points up as I was going in. Then BANG, BANG, BANG, Tipp (Tipperary) got three scores to draw level.

Suddenly, we were deep in crisis mode. This was similar to the drawn game with Galway in the Leinster final earlier this year. I drifted out to centre-forward, desperate to get the ball in my hand. I almost did, too, but Mickey Cahill just flicked it away and in a matter of seconds 'Bubbles' O'Dwyer was lining up that monster free into the Canal-End goal.

I fully expected him to score and was just desperate to get myself into the general area where Eoin Murphy's puck-out would be landing. They had to go to Hawk-Eye to establish that Bubbles's shot was fractions wide.

The final whistle, initially, left me with entirely selfish thoughts. When we had drawn the 2012 final, I departed the field, completely pumped by the performance I had just given. Now I was, it seemed, a three-minute man.

The replay proved much tighter than its predecessor. I took it upon myself to say a few words at half-time, as did Brian Hogan. I just mentioned how it reminded me of the 2002 All-Ireland semi-final against Tipperary with its sense that the game was there for us if we just upped things slightly.

The fact that both Hogie and I were comfortable speaking reflected just how tight the group had become. I can honestly say I do not remember a more united group hurling for Kilkenny in my time. The bond between young and old was really strong. I think it is what got us over the line.

I got on for Richie Hogan in the 58 minute. I did not manage to decorate those last twelve minutes of my inter-county career with anything especially spectacular. But I did feel involved again, I did feel part of the story. Richie Power got a critical goal shortly after my introduction and, almost instantly, his younger brother, John, drilled home another.

I went in to centre-forward, haring around the place, just trying to make my presence felt. My final act was to set up Colin Fennelly for the last score of the game, a beautiful feeling.

At the final whistle, all the emotional uncertainty I had experienced through the year just washed away. Standing there, as the first man to win ten All-Irelands, I was struck by the scale of the journey I had travelled from those childhood nights with my brother Paul. Imagining All-Irelands in the squash court at home. Those seconds, immediately after the final whistle, I will cherish for the rest of my days.

I lived the dream.

Paul O'Connell

Paul O'Connell was born in Limerick in 1979. He was selected for three British and Irish Lions rugby tours, including as captain in 2009. He won three Six Nations championships with Ireland, including two as captain, in 2014 and 2015; and he won two Heineken Cups with Munster.

In the following extract from his award-winning book *The Battle*, he reflects on coming back to the sport after a bad back injury.

The Battle

As a player in such a physical sport, what killed me were the injuries that stopped me from training. Forcing me to take steps back, just as I was getting where I needed to be. So instead of being like a pro cyclist who, at 30, has just gotten fitter and fitter over time, I ended up on this road where my fitness peaked and dipped. Injuries are part of the game, just as much as passing the ball or lifting weights. But a few of those injuries took so much rugby away from me. Just when I should have been at the top of my game, I was left feeling like I needed to make up for lost time.

I thought the announcement of my retirement would have been a footnote. That people would have been expecting it. And they would have said: 'Well look, that's been coming for a few years now – between this injury, that injury and the other injury.'

Before getting the epidural, I had considered surgery, but it was only the physical demands of rugby that were putting a strain on my back. I could pick up my son Paddy and swing him around without feeling anything.

To pass the time after getting the injection I watched twelve episodes of Californication, one after the other, because I needed to stay on my back. I had found that watching or reading anything about sport or high-performance training was making me feel more frustrated. They were constant reminders of what I was missing. The best thing for me was to switch off and give my body a chance to get better.

It was mid-November. I knew it was not a good idea to set myself a comeback date when nothing was certain about my recovery. But I needed something to focus on so I did it anyway. On 29 December, at the home game against Ulster, I tried everything and anything – magnets, massage therapy, hot-water bottles and yoga. It seemed like everyone I met had a story about their back. Christmas came and there was no improvement whatsoever.

People who find their jobs or their lives tough often think that other people are sailing through. It is rarely the case. I did not want to admit to anyone how I was feeling, mainly because I was trying hard to stay positive. When I got home after another day without progress, I would try to leave my frustration at the front door and be a decent husband and father.

I had bad days before with injuries, but I was never unhappy. It was a part of the game, and the challenge in front of me was to get right. But in the two weeks before Christmas, when I knew I had no hope of playing before the end of the year, I was lower than I'd ever been. My happiness level then was maybe three out of ten. Normally, it is ten out of ten. For the first few months of the season, I had been telling myself to give it time and do my rehab to the highest possible standard.

Six weeks after the epidural I had the same symptoms and no comeback date. I was very, very disillusioned. Going in for an hour's physiotherapy every day with my jeans on, because I did not have the heart to get into a tracksuit.

I had starting thinking about retirement. Figuring out what I would say if I was asked about it in an interview. With my injury profile, it would have been a fair question.

The following day I flew to London and saw a surgeon at the Lister Hospital, Damian Fahy. 'Looking at your scans,' he said, 'I think you could be back playing in six to eight weeks after an operation.'

As soon as he came out with that, my form was better. I was plotting my way back. When sport is your job and someone says you can be back on the field of play in six to eight weeks, what you hear is six.

Emily drove me to the Mater Hospital in Dublin at 6.45 on a Monday morning. New Year's Eve. I was on a trolley 20 minutes later. Just before they put me to sleep, I got a little bit emotional. But when I woke up, Keith Synnott was standing over me with a smile on his face, saying: 'It could not have gone any better.' I was on the comeback trail.

After a couple of weeks of lying flat on my back, I took my first steps outside the house. A short, slow walk to the local shop to buy a packet of Jelly Tots for Paddy. Over the following nights, I went further, listening to music with my hood up.

In the end, it took ten weeks before I had enough conditioning to get back on the pitch. But I never really doubted I would make the Harlequins game. What I did question, though, was whether we had it in us to win. The week before the quarter-final, in my second game back, we were murdered by Glasgow. It was a shocking performance. We conceded 51 points and gifted them tries.

Doug Howlett was out injured and I was captain for the Harlequins game. When I spoke to the media during the week, I was very down about our chances. I did not want to pretend any optimism. It was almost like I felt we needed an antidote to Rob Penney's relentless positivity. That we did not have the track record as a team to justify being in any way confident. I wanted us to be worried. I did not want to tell anyone it was going to be fine, because I did not know if it was. I wanted the new guys to be feeling the same kind of fear the old team had experienced, going over to Perpignan four years earlier, when we blew them away.

I could slag with the best of them in the gym, and a few of the lads noticed I was not my normal self.

'Is there no craic today?'

I just shook my head and gave them a half-smile. I did not tell people I was seriously worried. I was fearful of a 30 or 40 point drubbing (a serious defeat).

It was nothing to do with the game plan. I thought we could play any game we wanted within the framework Rob had given us.

At the end of the first half, on the halfway line, the referee signalled an advantage to Harlequins. They were six points ahead. Danny Care, their scrum-half, was looking at the referee, checking that it was a penalty. The second Jérôme Garcès blew the whistle, Care quick-tapped it. We knew it was coming. We had done the analysis. They had been scoring tries from that position all year. Conor Murray had already gone back ten metres. When he shot up and made the tackle, James Downey went in and poached it. It was a penalty to us.

I always thought those were the kind of moments that shifted the balance of power in games. It could have been a thirteen-point lead for them at half-time. But we'd spotted it, worked on stopping it and executed it brilliantly. Now we had pulled ourselves back from the brink. I was so proud. In that moment, I almost felt like we had won the competition.

About NALA

What is NALA?

The National Adult Literacy Agency (NALA) is a charity and membership based organisation. We work to ensure that adults with unmet literacy, numeracy and digital literacy needs can fully take part in society, and have access to learning opportunities that meet their needs.

We do this by:
- raising awareness of the importance of literacy;
- doing research and sharing good practice:
- providing online learning courses and a tutoring service;
- providing a Freephone support line;
- working in partnership with government departments, state agencies and others; and
- lobbying for further innovation and investment in adult literacy, numeracy and digital skills.

How can I improve my literacy, numeracy and digital literacy skills?

If you would like to improve your reading, writing, maths or technology skills we can help. Call us for free on **1800 20 20 65** or text **LEARN** to **50050**.

We are open from 9.30am to 5pm, Monday to Friday. Our service is confidential and we will talk to you about your learning options. You can:

- Learn with your local ETB adult literacy service; or
- Learn with NALA on the phone or online.

Or, you can do a combination of these.

All services are free and there are no exams.

Learn with your local ETB adult literacy service
- There are over 100 local adult literacy services around the country, run by Education and Training Boards (ETBs).
- You can attend your local service and work with trained tutors on a one-to-one basis or in small groups.

• The service is free.

For information on your nearest service, contact the NALA Freephone support line on **1800 20 20 65** or check out the NALA website at **www.nala.ie/find-a-centre.**

Learn with NALA
The National Adult Literacy Agency (NALA) has been offering phone and online tuition since 2000. The service is free and confidential and you decide what, where and how you want to learn.

There are two ways to learn with us and you can use both.

1. Learn with a tutor on the phone
We can work with you over the telephone, through the post or on the internet.

• You decide what to study. There is no set course.
• We call when it suits you – you just tell us when. There is no class schedule.

- Normally we make one call per week for up to 30 minutes.
- 5 days a week, early morning to late evening.
- We keep working with you until you meet your goals.

2. Learn online

We have a range of free, online courses from reading, writing and maths to career preparation and computer skills. You can learn at a pace that suits you and if you want, you can get a national Quality and Qualifications Ireland (QQI) qualification. See **www.learnwithnala.ie** for more information.

Adult Literacy is co-funded by the Government of Ireland and the European Social Fund.

Literacy needs in Ireland

The most recent OECD Survey of Adult Skills took place in 2012 and showed that in Ireland about one in six (18%) adults (between the ages of 16 and 65) struggle with reading and understanding everyday text. For example, reading a bus timetable or understanding medicine instructions. One in four adults (25%) struggle with using maths in everyday life. For example, basic addition, working out a bill or calculating percentages. The survey also showed that 42% of Irish adults struggle with basic digital tasks such as looking up a website or sending an email.

Literacy matters: Why we need to support literacy

Literacy is a human right to which every member of society is entitled. However only some members of our society have the literacy they need to flourish, thrive and reach their full potential.

Unmet literacy, numeracy and digital literacy needs can have a devastating impact on individuals, families and communities. People who have experienced educational and wider inequalities often earn less income, report poor health, are less likely to vote and struggle with accessing and understanding services and information.

Strong literacy, numeracy and digital skills enable adults, families and communities to engage effectively with public services and to understand and act upon new information. Stronger skills empower people to advocate for themselves and their communities, use technology and take part fully in society.

Check out the National Adult Literacy Agency's website **www.nala.ie** for more information on literacy in Ireland and how you can support our work.

Further Reading

The chapters of this book have been adapted and abridged from a number of brilliant sports autobiographies. If you are interested in reading more, you can find the names of all these books below.

- *Fight or Flight: My Life, My Choices*, Keith Earls with Tommy Conlon, Reach Sport, 2021
- *My Olympic Dream*, Katie Taylor, Simon & Schuster UK, 2012
- *Staying the Distance*, Ronnie Delany, O'Brien Press, 2006
- *From Ringsend to Tallaght*, Macdara Ferris and Eoghan Rice, 2021
- *The Choice*, Philly McMahon with Niall Kelly, Gill Books, 2017
- *Sonia: My Story*, Sonia O'Sullivan with Tom Humphries, Penguin Ireland, 2008
- *My Autobiography*, A.P. McCoy with Donn McLean, Orion, 2011
- *At the End of the Day*, by Paul Byrnes, Lettertec, 2021

- *Cyclone: My Story*, Barry McGuigan, Virgin Books, 2011
- *Game Changer*, Cora Staunton, Transworld Ireland, 2018
- *World Cup Diary*, Niall Quinn, New Island, 2004
- Speech made at Eid celebration at Croke Park, Bonnar Ó Loingsigh, 2020
- *Driven*, Rosemary Smith with Ann Ingle, Harper Collins, 2018
- *The Autobiography*, Henry Shefflin, Penguin Ireland, 2015
- *The Battle*, Paul O'Connell with Alan English, Penguin Ireland, 2015

Acknowledgements

New Island would like to thank the Department of Rural and Community Development and the Department of Further and Higher Education, Research, Innovation and Science for supporting this book.

We are also grateful to our partners at NALA and to our series editor Patricia Scanlan, whose unfailing energy and generosity of spirit has driven the Open Door series forward since 1998.

Last but not least, we would like to thank the athletes and rightsholders of the material reproduced in this book, who have kindly collaborated with us to make their words available in plain English. Specifically:

- Extract from *Fight or Flight* by Keith Earls, published by Reach Sport. Reprinted by permission of Reach Publishing Services Ltd. Copyright © 2021 Keith Earls.
- Extract from *My Olympic Dream* by Katie Taylor, published by Simon & Schuster UK. Reprinted by

permission of Simon & Schuster. Copyright © 2012 Katie Taylor.

- Extract from *Staying the Distance* by Ronnie Delany published by The O'Brien Press. Reprinted by permission of The O'Brien Press Ltd, Dublin. Copyright © 2006 Ronnie Delany.
- Extract from *From Ringsend to Tallaght* edited by Macdara Ferris and Eoin Rice. Reprinted by permission of the editors. Copyright © 2021 Gavin Bazunu.
- Extract from *The Choice* by Philly McMahon published by Gill Books. Reproduced by permission of M.H. Gill & Co. Copyright © 2017, 2018 Philly McMahon.
- Extract from *Sonia: My Story* by Sonia O'Sullivan published by Penguin Ireland. Reprinted by permission of Penguin Books Ltd. Copyright © 2008 Sonia O'Sullivan.
- Extract from *My Autobiography* by A.P. McCoy, published by Orion Publishing. Reprinted by permission of Orion Publishing Ltd through PLSclear. Copyright © 2011 A.P. McCoy.
- Extract from *At the End of the Day* by Paul Byrnes, published by Lettertec. Reprinted by permission of Paul Byrnes Media. Copyright © 2021 Paul Byrnes.
- Extract from *Cyclone* by Barry McGuigan published by Virgin Books. Reprinted by permission of The Random House Group Ltd. Copyright © 2011 Barry McGuigan.
- Extract from *Game Changer* by Cora Staunton published by Transworld Ireland. Reprinted by permission of The Random House Group Ltd. Copyright © 2018 Cora Staunton.

LEGENDS

- Speech made by Bonnar Ó Loingsigh at Eid celebration at Croke Park, July 2020. Reprinted by permission of Bonnar Ó Loingsigh. Copyright © 2020 Bonnar Ó Loingsigh.
- Extract from *Driven* by Rosemary Smith. Reprinted by permission of HarperCollins Publishers Ltd, Copyright © 2018 Rosemary Smith.
- Extract from *The Autobiography* by Henry Shefflin published by Penguin Ireland. Reprinted by permission of Penguin Books Ltd. Copyright © 2015 Henry Shefflin.
- Extract from *The Battle* by Paul O'Connell published by Penguin Ireland. Reprinted by permission of Penguin Books Ltd. Copyright © 2016 Paul O'Connell.